CHECHNYA

ALSO BY ANDREW MEIER

Black Earth: A Journey Through Russia After the Fall

CHECHNYA

TO THE HEART
OF A CONFLICT

ANDREW MEIER

W. W. NORTON & COMPANY

NEW YORK LONDON

Grateful acknowledgment is made for permission to reprint lines from *Hadji Murad,* in Leo Tolstoy, *Master and Man and Other Stories,* Penguin Classics, 1977, translated by Paul Foote.

The chapters in this book appeared in Andrew Meier's *Black Earth: A Journey Through Russia After the Fall*

For information about permission to reproduce selections from this book, write to Permissions, W. W. Norton & Company, Inc., 500 Fifth Avenue, New York, NY 10110

Manufacturing by the Haddon Craftsmen, Inc.

ISBN 0-393-32732-9 (pbk.)

W. W. Norton & Company, Inc., 500 Fifth Avenue, New York, N.Y. 10110
www.wwnorton.com

W. W. Norton & Company Ltd., Castle House, 75/76 Wells Street, London W1T 3QT

1 2 3 4 5 6 7 8 9 0

In memoriam

AUTHOR'S NOTE

One can transliterate the Russian language into Latin script variously. I have elected not to use the American scholarly standard, the Library of Congress system, in the hope of rendering the Russian as readable and recognizable as possible. (As such, the reader will find "Yeltsin" and not "El'tsin.") With regard to translations, I have sought to use existing English texts whenever possible. Only when such translations do not exist or fall short of the Russian have I resorted to my own. Lastly, in a few rare cases, to protect the safety of individuals I have substituted names.

The way home was through a fallow field of black earth which had just been ploughed. I walked along the dusty, gently rising black-earth road. The ploughed field was squire's land and very large, so that on either side of the road and on up the slope you could see nothing but black evenly furrowed fallow land, as yet unharrowed. The ploughing was well done and there was not a plant or blade of grass to be seen across the whole field: it was all black. What a cruel, destructive creature man is. How many different living creatures and plants he has destroyed in order to support his own life, I thought, instinctively looking for some sign of life in the midst of this dead black field.

–Leo Tolstoy, *Hadji Murad*

CHECHNYA

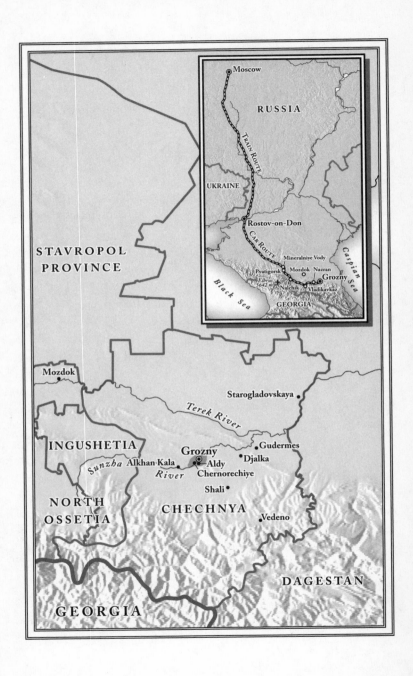

STAVROPOL
PROVINCE

RUSSIA

UKRAINE

TRAIN ROUTE

Rostov-on-Don

CAR ROUTE

Mineralniye Vody

Pyatigorsk   Mozdok   Nazran
Elbrus   Grozny
5642 m   Nalchik
                        Vladikavkaz

Black Sea

GEORGIA

Caspian Sea

Moscow

Mozdok

Starogladovskaya

Terek River

INGUSHETIA

Sunzha   Alkhan-Kala

River

Grozny

Aldy

Chernorechiye

Djalka

Gudermes

NORTH
OSSETIA

Shali

CHECHNYA

Vedeno

GEORGIA

DAGESTAN

INTRODUCTION

IT BEGAN WITH THE PLANES. On the night of August 24, 2004, nearly thirteen years to the day after the failed coup attempt against Mikhail Gorbachev, two Tupelov airliners disappeared, within minutes of one another, from the skies over Russia. A farmer near Rostov, years out of work and accustomed to the silence of the steppe, awoke to the buckle of noise. The sky had filled with a burst of light, he told the correspondent from state television. By daylight, the Russian authorities sought to cover up the cause, but all Russia knew the truth. A new season of terror had begun.

In the days that followed, it emerged that the planes had been blown up–two Chechen women, the authorities would claim once they had pieced the evidence together, had traveled from Grozny, the Chechen capital, to a Moscow airport on a suicide mission. A week later, another Chechen woman walked beside a metro station in the center of Moscow, and just as the masses of commuters streamed out into the warm air, detonated a bomb, killing herself and taking ten innocents with her. All three were *shakhidki*–female suicide bombers bent on martyrdom, the newest soldiers in the Chechen resistance.

Then came Beslan, the most horrific attack yet. In the far-off capitals of the West, the realm Russians have taken to calling "the civilized world," the headlines would scream in shock. The terrorists had descended to a circle of evil without precedent. To target a school–taking hostage more than a thousand innocent civilians, the majority of them women and children, was a nadir in the annals of terrorism. Russians watched the climax of the fifty-two-hour siege at Middle School Number One in horror. They remembered their Dostoyevsky. Etched in the collective memory was Ivan Karamazov's nihilist dictum: he could not believe in any God who would allow children to suffer at the hand of sadists.

We may never know the identities of all the men who held the school in North Ossetia hostage. At first, the FSB, the post-Soviet heirs of the KGB, said that "ten Arabs" had taken part in the attack. Vladimir Putin even repeated the claim, before his defense minister, Sergei Ivanov, a fellow KGB alumnus and the president's closest confidante, refuted it. Among the terrorists' corpses identified, Ivanov said, there were no Chechens. Yet that statement too, in the days that followed, was amended. Like the implausible turns of a Gogol short story, the Kremlin line seemed forever shifting, an account under construction with each new proclamation.

Under pressure, Putin made a rare concession: he vowed to open the siege's disastrous resolution—the deaths of more than 350 civilians, half of them children—to an inquiry. Even in the loyal hands of the upper house of the Russian parliament, the investigation would mark a first for Russian history. In the wake of the seizure of the Moscow theater in the fall of 2002, when all 41 terrorists were killed but 130 hostages died from a military gas, Putin rejected any public reckoning. Instead, he promised an internal accounting that, somewhere in the years since it quietly stalled, was never to be completed.

Westerners look to a parliamentary inquiry and hope that the tragedy of Beslan may yield a salient lesson. Russians, however, being Russian, and still suffering the sins of Kremlin rulers past, have little faith in the state's powers of self-examination. Putin, they knew, would rage on about the toll of terror. But the families of the hundreds who died at Beslan, and the millions of Russians who now faced a new fear from St. Petersburg to Vladivostok, expected little to change. The state would redraw its hard line across Chechnya, proclaim yet again a promise of protection, and, all too predictably, leave the survivors alone to search for solace. Putin, at the same time, in the name of the antiterrorism fight, would grab yet more power.

RUSSIA'S TROUBLES with Chechnya, despite what Putin and his appeasers in the West would claim, did not begin with September 11. The Chechens have yearned for freedom since the days of Catherine the Great. The present troubles have flitted on and off America's television screens for a decade now. On November 26, 1994, Boris Yeltsin and the heirs of the KGB staged a proxy attack in Grozny against the wayward province's newly risen separatist ruler, a recently retired Soviet air force general named Djokhar Dudayev. As the Soviet monolith disintegrated, and independence movements rent the old empire, Dudayev had come home to lead a rebellion. In late 1991, backed by a crew that was part criminal, part partisan, and all nationalist, he unilaterally proclaimed an independent Chechen republic.

Moscow's counterinsurgency proved hapless and bloody, a post-Soviet Bay of Pigs. Yet it was only a prelude to the onslaught that followed. On December 31, 1994, when Yeltsin then sent hundreds of tanks into the center of Grozny, the "first" war commenced. It would be, Yeltsin was assured, "a small, victorious war," in the words of a minister under the Romanovs. It was a campaign of blundering Russian generals and ardent Chechen guerrillas, waged with little attention on either side to the niceties of the Geneva Conventions. For the Russians, the war soon turned into a costly, and deeply unpopular, quagmire. In 1996, a Russian provincial governor would circulate a petition demanding its end, and promptly collect a million signatures. For the Chechens, however, it was a war of infinite passion and pride. It was a time of ascendant heroes, men who rose from obscurity to find fame in the bloodshed. Men like Shamil Basayev, a young commander born under Khrushchev, and named in honor of the Caucasus's most fabled warrior, Imam Shamil, leader of the mountaineers' nineteenth-century campaigns against the tsars.

The first campaign would end in 1996, with a desperate cease-fire. The truce was called in the town of Khasavyurt, in the neighboring republic of Dagestan. The Khasavyurt Accords brought a measure of stability, but both parties had skirted the critical question of sovereignty, leaving it to be determined in five years' time. Chechnya, in the years that followed, gained the veneer of de facto independence, but the central question of status lingered.

Aslan Maskhadov, a former Chechen field commander, and Soviet artillery officer, was elected president of the new Chechen Republic of Ichkeria, as the triumphant separatists christened their homeland. But no one, save the Taliban in Afghanistan, gave the statelet official recognition. Islamic jurisprudence would be introduced–*Shari'a* courts and public lashings. Separated by an economic quarantine from the rest of the Russian Federation, the local GDP seemed driven by the kidnapping trade. The interregnum lasted a volatile three years, as the republic languished without any genuine legal, economic, or law enforcement infrastructure. The Chechens had won the day, but their homeland had devolved into a lawless enclave, a magnet for Islamist extremists, and a time-bomb in the center of the North Caucasus.

Before the war, few Chechens would have claimed their version of Islam, so thoroughly diluted by seven decades of Soviet atheism, was orthodox. The principal rules and regulations of society were set by *adat*, the Chechens' centuries-old customary law. The years of war would change all that. During the republic's isolation, Moscow did all it could to undermine the Maskhadov regime, while the Russian General Staff, humiliated by the retreat from the south, yearned for a grudge match. In the vacuum, a new religious force took hold–Wahhabism, the austere strain of Islam that emanates from Saudi Arabia. Its teachers, in the main, were young men with long beards, stern gazes, and shadowy sources of funding. On the scorched earth of Chechnya, among a generation raised on war and little else, the movement found a fast and impassioned following.

If in the first war, the Chechen rebels were freedom fighters in the Reagan mold, yearning for independence in a classic war of decolonization, the war that began anew in late 1999–Putin's War that continues to this day–marked a sharp turn. It began with the invasion by forces from Chechnya into Dagestan to the east, and the series of apartment bombings in Moscow and two other Russian cities. The sparks that reignited the conflict, and provided a welcome platform to catapult an unknown retired KGB lieutenant colonel to Yeltsin's throne, are detailed in the pages that follow. But whatever its cause, the "second" Chechen war differed markedly from the first. For the Russians, the new campaign would be even more brutal, with far more troops, sorties, and bombs. For the Chechens, in turn, the talk of sovereignty now gave way to an urge for little but revenge. And among the most militant, as Russia entered the twenty-first century under Putin, the rebellion in Chechnya would take on a new name, jihad.

NO ONE CAN JUSTIFY TERRORISM, of any species. Neither can anyone explain mass murder, whether sponsored by a state or a half-crazed gang of criminals or soldiers. It is beyond the powers of reason to comprehend how men could shoot children in the back. That is not to say we should not try.

Under Putin, Russia remains a land in upheaval. There are troubles with restive oligarchs, old epidemics of corruption and alcoholism, new ones of HIV and tuberculosis. Chechnya, however, remains the wound that unites the country in anguish. The true tally of the dead will never be known–

more than one hundred thousand combining both sides is the modest estimate. The Kremlin has called the attack at Beslan "Russia's 9/11." The Russian president has looked to Washington and pledged to adopt George W. Bush's doctrine of "preemption." The Chechens, to be sure, have won no friends by the recent campaign of terror. But Putin, too, has yielded no ground, steadfastly refusing to concede that his prosecution of the war could have fueled the rebel fire.

Putin did not start the war in Chechnya. He inherited it from his enfeebled predecessor. However, under his tenure the conflict has become far more radicalized and militant. Only under Putin did the Chechens devise a new weapon: suicide bombers bent on killing as many Russian civilians as possible. In June 2000, during the first summer of his reign, and days before I entered the republic, the first Chechen *shakhidka* blew herself up, detonating a truck bomb at an army checkpoint. By now, the evidence is clear: the Kremlin's unyielding policy, coupled with the ineptitude and brutality of its armed forces, has only played to the hand of its most radicalized opponents. Shamil Basayev—now Russia's most wanted man—first fought alongside the Moscow-backed insurgents in the 1992 war in Abkhazia, the breakaway Muslim province in Georgia. Today Basayev, who claimed credit for the Moscow theater siege and is commander of the female suicide brigades, signs his public communiqués Abdallah Shamil Abu-Idris, the leader of the Islamic Brigade of Martyrs, the self-proclaimed Riyadh as-Salihiin (the Gardens of the Righteous).

This is a report from Chechnya, not a history of the republic nor a primer on its recent turmoil. It first appeared as the record of one leg of successive travels across Russia. In my book, *Black Earth: A Journey Through Russia After the Fall*, I followed the cardinal points of the compass to the country's extremes in search of a portrait of the nation a decade after the Soviet collapse. As such, it is one reporter's journey, an account bound by time and place. In offering it, I have but one modest aim. My hope is that it may become a resource, a map that helps readers to trace the convulsions that have led to the present depravity.

–Andrew Meier
New York City
September 11, 2004

ONE

WE WERE, AT LONG LAST, on the outskirts of Aldy, an ancient village of overgrown fruit trees and low-slung tin roofs on the southern edge of Grozny, the Chechen capital, and Issa was singing, "*Moi gorod Groooozny, ya po tebe skuchaaayu . . . no ya k tebe vernuuus, moi gorod Grozny moi.*"

He was an imposing figure, just over six feet, his chest and shoulders so broad he appeared taller. Issa liked to keep his silvering hair shaved on the sides of his head and at the back of his neck. The cut lent him the stern air of a military man or a Soviet bureaucrat of stature, an image, as was no doubt the intent, to intimidate at the checkpoints. More often silent, Issa broke into song when the air around him grew too quiet. Now, just as the roadblock, the last one before Aldy, rose into view, Issa was singing at the top of his lungs.

"*Moi gorod Groooozny,*" he wailed. "My city, the city of Grozny, oh, how I miss you, but I shall return to you. . . ."

There were four of us in the rattling Soviet Army jeep, known endearingly as a UAZik, pronounced *wahzik*, in the common parlance. Lord knows what image we projected to the well-muscled, sunburned, and deeply suspicious Russian soldiers at the checkpoints. Sometimes they were drunk. Nearly always they were scared. In Chechnya, I'd learned, checkpoints were the measure of one's day. People did not ask, "How far it is?" but "How many checkpoints are there?" Each day we crossed at least a dozen.

On this sweltering morning in July, we had already passed seventeen. The posts were the center of activity amid the ruins of the city. Conscripts maintained the constant vigil, checking the cars and their passengers, while their officers, hands on radios, sat in shaded huts off the road. But this post was nearly empty, and the OMON officer who stopped us, a pit bull from Irkutsk, was not in a good mood. His arms and neck glowed with the burned pink skin of a new arrival. He wore wraparound sunglasses and a bandanna over his shaved head. Tattoos, the proud emblems of Russian soldiers and prisoners, covered his biceps. "*Slava*" ("glory") adorned the right one. It could be a name or a desire. He wore no shirt, only a green vest fitted with grenades, a knife, and magazine clips to feed the Kalashnikov he held firmly in both hands. His fingers seemed soldered to it.

We may have looked legit, but we were a fraud. Issa ostensibly was a ranking member of the wartime administration in Chechnya, the Russians' desperate attempt at governance in the restive republic of Muslims, however lapsed, Sovietized, and secularized. He had the documents to prove it, but the man who signed them had since been fired. Issa knew the life span of his documents was limited. At any checkpoint his "client," as he had taken to calling me, could be pulled from the jeep, detained, interrogated, and packed off on the next flight to Moscow.

At fifty-one, Issa boasted a résumé that revealed the successful climb of a Chechen apparatchik. Born in Central Asian exile, in Kyrgyzstan, five years after Stalin had deported the Chechens in 1944, he had graduated from the Grozny Oil Institute in 1971. For twenty-one years he worked at Grozneft, the Chechen arm of the Soviet Oil and Gas Ministry. He spent the last Soviet years, until Yeltsin clambored onto the tank in 1991, in western Siberia, overseeing the drilling of oil wells in Tyumen. He spoke a smattering of French, a bit of Arabic, and a dozen words in English—all learned, he liked to tease, during stints in Iraq and Syria.

As the Soviet Union collapsed, life went sour fast. Djokhar Dudayev—the Soviet Air Force general who was to lead the stand against Moscow—returned to Grozny, and the fever for independence seized the capital. Issa, then a director of one of Chechnya's biggest chemical plants, took up arms against the insurgents. In the fall of 1993, more than a year before Yeltsin first sent troops into Chechnya, with Moscow's backing Issa and his fellow partisans rallied around a former Soviet petrochemicals minister and staged a pathetic attempt to overthrow Dudayev.[1]

He was careful not to dispense details, but the scars were hard to hide. His right forearm had a golf ball–size hole, remnants of a bullet taken on the opposition's line north of Grozny in September 1993. The bullet had pierced his arm and lodged in his left shoulder. A few months later Dudayev's freedom fighters got him again. Kalashnikov fire had ripped his stomach, intestine, and lungs, leaving a horrific gnarl of tissue in the center of his body. He'd moved his family—a wife, two boys, and a girl—to Moscow.

But he wanted to be clear: He never wanted to fight. "We never loved the Russians," he said. "We just hated that corrupt little *mafiya* shit." He was speaking of Dudayev, the fallen independence leader, the man many Chechens, much younger and more devout, now called the founding martyr of the separatist Islamic state, the Chechen Republic of Ichkeria, as Dudayev had ordered his native land rechristened.[2]

In front of me, behind the wheel, sat Yura. Projecting a genuine sweetness, he was a good-looking kid with blue-green eyes and blond hair that his mother cut short each week with a straight razor. He had thin cheeks, covered with freckles and shaded by the beginnings of a beard. Just twenty-two, he was lucky to have made it this far. He belonged to one of the world's most unfortunate species; he was an ethnic Russian born in Chechnya. "Our Mowgli," Issa had jibed, equating Yura with Kipling's jungle boy. Everyone laughed. There was no need to explain. Mowgli was raised by wolves. The Chechens, centuries ago, had made the wolf their mascot, the embodiment of their struggle.

The last of the crew, bouncing beside me in the back seat of the car, was Shvedov. It was a last name—few ever learned his first—that meant "the Swede." There was nothing, however, Swedish about him. He had a tanned bald head and a scruffy dirty brown beard and mustache. He carried an ID from the magazine the *Motherland*, but his paid vocation was what is known in the field as a fixer. For decades he earned a living, or something approximating it, by getting reporters in and out of places they had no business being in. Usually genial and often hilarious, he could be brilliant. But Shvedov's greatest attribute was that he did not drink. I had known him for years but never traveled with him. After only three days I discovered my own heretofore unknown homicidal urges coming on strong. Somehow I had missed Shvedov's worst sin: He talked without pause. (When he did not talk, he clacked his upper dentures incessantly on a set of lower teeth blackened by a lifetime of unfiltered Russian tobacco.) A colleague who traveled with him often had offered a tip: "Keep a cigarette in his mouth." But even smoking, Shvedov talked.

THE SIBERIAN PIT BULL barked at Yura. "Turn off the car," he instructed. Issa politely tried to ply his documents, but the soldier would have none of it. "Forget your papers, old man," he shouted. Shvedov, seeing the worst coming, proffered his press card from the *Motherland*. The OMON officer from Irkutsk had never heard of the honored Soviet monthly, which Shvedov insisted still existed, even though its readership could no longer afford to subscribe. "Stay in the car," the officer yelled at the insistent bald man in front of him, before turning his sights on me.

"Get out," he then commanded me.

One thing I'd learned about checkpoints long ago was it was best not to get out—ever. By now we had been stopped so often a routine had formed. A soldier would approach, profanities would rain, we would offer documents, another soldier would lean closer, we would wait, and then, the formalities exhausted, we would be waved through. Silence, I had learned, was the best policy. But this fellow wanted me out of the UAZik. He yelled again. He wanted to frisk the car, search its innards, rummage our bags. I tried to demur. I offered to help.

Undeterred, he opened the door and, with his Kalashnikov, nudged me aside. He lifted the seats, opened the metal canisters underneath, and, maintaining his silence, rifled our bags. When he was done, he grunted and jumped from the UAZik. Yura sat frozen until Issa ordered him, through his teeth, to turn the key, turn the goddamned key. As we moved on, I watched the soldier retreat to his roadside squalor, half a tent strung to a tree and a broken chair posted in the hot sun. With his back to us, he flicked his left hand sharply through the air, as if to swat an insect. We were beneath him.

We drove on, numb to everything but the sun, the dust, the bumps. Issa had stopped singing. Only the roar of the helicopters overhead accompanied us, and then, suddenly, as we turned off the road, the silence returned. We had entered a village without discernible life. No cars, no people. The first trees were tall, bare stumps, their branches shorn long ago. Then yards, all untended, their green veils grown too thick or too thin. Everywhere the branches, heavy with fruit, hung low. The season had come, but no one was picking. Everywhere there was only the weight of the still air. We had arrived.

I had marked Aldy, this Chechen village, on the map of Chechnya I had bought on a Moscow street corner months earlier. Aldy was the destination I'd set myself and shared with no one when I began the journey to the south. Something horrific, unspeakable, had happened here five months before. On a cold Saturday in midwinter, Russian forces had committed one of the bloodiest of the Chechnya massacres in this village. No one will ever know the true body count, but in Aldy on February 5, 2000, Russian soldiers had summarily executed at least sixty civilians.

A half circle of a dozen Chechen men, some lean and strong, others gray and bent over, huddled in a caucus as we drove in. Yura parked the UAZik across the road from them. They did not move from the lonely shade. One man, young, fit, and prominently armed, gripped the Kalashnikov on his shoulder. He wore full camouflage and tiny sunglasses. He could have been on either side, a fighter loyal to the rebels or a Chechen police officer in the Russians' employ. Issa didn't like the look of the sunglasses.

I got out, alone, and walked toward the men. One of the older men was separating leaves from a thin branch in his hands. As I approached, the young Chechen stepped forward. In his hands was the AK-47, shiny and new. Strapped across his chest was a leather bandolier, bulging with clips, grenades, and a pair of wooden-handled knives. A century and a half earlier Alexandre Dumas *père* had noted the Chechens' love of weaponry during a romantic romp across the Caucasus in 1858, a time when the Chechens struggled against the tsar. "All these mountain fighters are fanatically brave," wrote the creator of *The Three Musketeers*, "and whatever money they acquire is spent on weapons. A Chechen . . . may be literally in rags, but his sword, dagger and gun are of the finest quality."[3]

I told the armed man that I was a journalist, an American. I'd come to talk to people who were here the day "they" came. We did not shake hands, but he nodded and shifted the rifle from his hands to his shoulder. "Walk with me," he said. The sunglasses, their gold frame catching the sun, covered his eyes. Slowly we crossed the dirt road and headed away from the jeep, away from my guides, away from the Chechen men standing against the wall of metal gates and fences.

Oddly, a calm enveloped me. I kept walking, afraid to lose pace. Three options formed in my mind. This fellow is taking you around the corner, just out of sight of your companions, where you'll be summarily executed; or he's intent on kidnapping you, leading you to a house nearby to be sold on down the road from there; or he's bringing you to see someone—an elder?—who will listen to your best introduction and then either bless your presence in the village or send you away.

I had come to Aldy prepared. By March an amateur video, forty-six minutes long, made by the villagers had surfaced in Moscow. It featured corpses and widows. I had interviewed the lucky ones; the survivors who'd made it out. I had studied the reports, detailed and methodical, of the human rights activists. But I wanted to learn more than the extent of the massacre. I wanted to understand the motivation behind the horror. Aldy was not, as an American diplomat, a man of high rank and expertise in Russia, had tried to convince me, "just another case of Russian heavy-handedness." It was a conspicuous illustration, in miniature, of Russia's military onslaught in Chechnya.

The young Chechen led me on. But even before we reached the gate of the house, a wave of relief hit, and my shoulders settled. I knew where we were going. I had memorized a hand-drawn map of Aldy's long streets. We were calling on the man the fortunate ones had told me to see first, Shamkhan, the village mullah.

TWO

CHECHNYA LIES A THOUSAND miles south of Moscow, between the Black and Caspian Seas. Weeks before, I had opted for the slow route south. On an airless Moscow afternoon early in a summer of record temperatures, I boarded the *Quiet Don*, the North Caucasus express bound for Rostov-on-Don, nearly twenty hours to the south. From Rostov, the threshold to the Caucasus, I was to drive on across the steppes before coming to the foothills of the mountains and crossing into Chechnya. It was not the beaten path. Deadlines forced most correspondents to fly from Moscow to Nazran, the capital of neighboring Ingushetia, the tiny republic with the closest airport to Grozny. But I wanted to proceed slowly, to see the land that stretched between Moscow and Grozny, to mark the gradual descent into the lands of kidnapping, war, and a fast-evolving faith in Islam.

Like nearly every Russian, I knew something of the journey before it began. Tales of the Caucasus—martial epics featuring swarthy mountaineers with bejeweled daggers and mysterious black-eyed lasses—featured prominently in the nineteenth-century imagination. For Pushkin, and Mikhail Lermontov after him, the Caucasus was an exotic land to be envied, a realm free of the strictures of tsarist society. Both Pushkin and Lermontov, the poet and writer best known for *A Hero of Our Time*, were exiled to the south. Tolstoy went voluntarily. For young Tolstoy, the Caucasus proved a martial and moral training ground. In Chechnya he saw his first battle, wrote his first story, and heard a tale he remembered his entire life and returned to in his last work of fiction, *Hadji Murad*. Nearly a century after Tolstoy's death, relations between Moscow and the "small nations," the belittling term Soviet officialdom used for the peoples of the Caucasus, had grown only worse. Yet even among Russians, their name for the lands—Kavkaz—rarely failed to conjure, in its two clipped syllables that rose like a gallop, a romantic genie.

The Kazan station teemed so with sweating multitudes that I nearly missed the train. Inside, I found Kolya, lying on the opposite bunk in our narrow cabin. He was a bear of a man with a mop of ginger hair. Only hours later, once we'd emptied a bottle of Dagestani cognac, and Zhenka, the round-cheeked dining car girl, had thrice come and gone, delivering plates of glabrous chicken and half-fried potatoes, did I learn his last name.

"Nabokov," he said, without an inkling anyone had ever shared the name.

Freckles covered Kolya's red skin, and his left shoulder was tattooed with twin mountain peaks. "Mount Ararat," he said, rubbing a meaty palm over the skin. He had served in the Soviet border guards in Armenia, then a decade in the coal mines of the Don Basin—until the mines started closing. "Gorbachev," he said of the days when everything suddenly changed. "Glasnost, all that." When the work ran out, he'd gone to the far end of the empire, to mine gold in Magadan, once home to the Kolyma fields, the primary source of Russia's rosy gold, and the Gulag's largest labor camps. He lasted only a couple of years in the Far East, before coming home. Back in Rostov, he moved into the new world, "cooperatives," the Soviets' last-ditch experiment at small semiprivate enterprise.

Those were wild but good days, especially once he got to know the Chechens. "Best people in the whole union," Kolya declared. For years he'd partnered only with Chechens. They had joined forces in trade, jewelry, and electronics in the years before the war. He didn't know about now, but back then the Chechens were his best friends. "They'd do anything for me, and I'd do anything for them." He could not say the same of his fellow Russians.

"Walk into a Chechen's house," Kolya said, "and you are in his protection. I wouldn't suggest trying it in Moscow."

For a time we sat in silence, opposite each other on the hard bunks. We let the rhythmic clank of metal on metal fill the cabin. Beyond our curtained window, figures appeared in the blurred rush beside the rails: drunken wanderers roused to consciousness by passing thunder; Gypsy families bedding down in a dusky field; a babushka on a shortcut through the woods, the day's haul slung across her back. Even as the sun set, the temperature ran high. The window, however, remained locked shut. It did not matter. In such moments, I realized, as Kolya returned to the Chechens, there are few places in the world where strangers can find such closeness, with such ease, as on a Russian train.

We talked for hours. Kolya was not optimistic on the war. "They're not ones to give up," he said, looking into the woods. The pines and firs were aflame in the midsummer sunset. The musty compartment had caught the glow. "Chechens don't like to be screwed. This is no longer about independence. This is about revenge, honor, and this is forever." Before long the sun disappeared, and the cognac with it. Our little table grew crowded. Beer bottles swayed amid the plates of half-eaten chicken. Zhenka had warmed to Kolya. She now stopped by every time she delivered another meal to the far end of the train. Her cheeks red, and her brow aglow with sweat, she sat on the edge of Kolya's bunk, moving closer to him with each visit. As the hours passed, their giggling turned to laughter and then, as the last bottle emptied, to silence. Outside, as the woods gave way to black fields, the figures beside the tracks grew fewer and in the darkness lost distinction.

I managed a few hours' sleep before Kolya's snoring woke me. It was early morning, but we had reached someplace far from Moscow. Overnight, the world beyond our window had turned pastoral. In the first sun of the morning, we passed men baling hay, shirtless boys playing daredevil on Ural motorcycles, children swimming in rivulets in their underwear, brigades of large women weeding between the rails, old men fishing. The lands to the south may follow a farmer's schedule, but commerce seemed to center on the train. In the stations, men elbowed one another to board the cars and offer dried fish and vodka, while the babushkas lined the platforms, squatting behind buckets of apricots and walnuts, cherries and raspberries.

Kolya awoke with a groan just as we passed the town where he had mined coal, Shakhtnaya (Mining Town). At the station's edge a cluster of young men, their heads shaved, gathered by an olive gray army truck. Parents stood beside them, fussing. A farewell. One man pumped an accordion, while his wife clutched two bottles. They sang their son onto the train, through the corridor, and into a cabin down the way. In a moment the train jerked back to movement, and the forlorn parents barely escaped. At the end of the short platform a young couple kissed. They sat on a low wall of concrete under a weeping willow. The girl had tucked her knees up, beneath a long white skirt.

Kolya belched and stretched. He'd taken the train up to Moscow from Rostov only the day before. He'd been in the capital just a few hours, to visit "the big brother." His older brother had served in the KGB, first in Leningrad, then in East Germany. Now he'd been given a big job in the Kremlin. The résumé was strangely familiar. Putin had followed the same career path. Kolya had gone to Moscow, he said once we were well into the cognac, to get his brother's blessing. A deal was cooking. He needed a Kremlin seal to nail it down. He did not elaborate. He was just happy his brother had consented so fast. They'd had plenty of time to go to a big restaurant, just off Red Square. They'd gorged themselves. Kolya loved his brother and revered him. "Even up there," he said, pointing to the grimy ceiling above us, "he's still just like me, a normal guy from a shitty little town in the provinces."

THREE

ROSTOV STRADDLES THE broad waters of the Don. I climbed off the train and immediately felt the change in latitude. Everywhere the Caucasus announced itself. Dust-cloaked trains disgorged the pilgrims from across the steppes—Armenians and Georgians, Cossacks and Azeris, Ossetians and plenty of weary Russians. In the station the morning heat was spiced by the gristly shashlik and warm lavash piled high on wooden carts. The sweet smells betrayed the proximity of the mountainous lands to the south. So, too, did the OMON patrols, the stern officers who lined the exits, checking the documents of each new arrival before he or she could step into their city.

Rostov was not only the crossroads of the Caucasus in Russia but the last foothold of state power in the south. "The last Russian city," Kolya had called it, offering less of an acclamation than a warning of what lay farther south. "Beyond Rostov," he added, "it's only them." The OMON officers, sweating as they failed to keep pace with the elbowing hordes, betrayed their own fear, the anxiety that had stalked the city since the first urgings for independence stirred among the "small nations" of the south.

Rostov had long been a bulwark of Russian power. The narrow streets of its oldest neighborhoods were lined with nineteenth-century red brick merchants' houses from a past era. The filigreed roofs and wooden porches leaned with age but struggled to retain an elegant bearing. Once best known for its tractor plant, the USSR's largest, Rostov in recent years had gained fame as the unlikely breeding ground for one of Russia's most notorious serial killers. The 1994 prosecution of Andrei Chikatilo, murderer of at least fifty-two, became the first celebrity murder trial in the former Soviet Union. Theories abounded on why the city of sleepy hills and idled collective farmers had produced such homicidal intemperance. Explanations swirled but as always, never settled with any certainty.

Even before the advent of "the Rostov Ripper," the city had carried a reputation for crime–specifically, an illicit trade in just about anything. Odessa, went the old line, was the mama of Soviet crime, and Rostov the papa. Now the crime Lenin called speculation was known as *biznes*, and the city teemed with crowds buying and selling. The automobile market, one of the largest in Russia, stretched for miles. Moscow had its own sprawling open-air bazaars, where big-shouldered babushkas vied with Caucasian traders, but for any trader working Russia's southern reaches, Rostov was the dream.

The crossroads lured not only pilgrims from across the mountains, but a blond, blue-eyed Englishman raised and bred, as he put it, for the financial markets of London. John Warren had lived in the city on the Don for years. Brash and pink in the cheek, he seemed an eternal English public school boy, better suited to the world of Evelyn Waugh than Maksim Gorky. Yet in an unlikely post-Soviet evolution, Warren had risen fast in the turmoil of the new market–from a Moscow apprenticeship in the empire of Marc Rich, the elusive American financier living in Switzerland, to his current position as the honorary consul of Her Majesty's Government at the edge of the Russian steppes.

Warren had cause to be pleased with himself. He'd married a Russian beauty and fathered, a year or two back, a blond Sasha. He was fond of reiterating his conviction, gained by experience, that "Russia can work!" His service to the queen, albeit unsalaried, allowed him to affix a miniature Union Jack to the antenna of his Land Rover, an army green Defender, and to ensure, or so he hoped, his own small stake in the local economy. Warren was something of a local celebrity. He wore white shorts and dark sunglasses and careered around in the Defender, the only one in town. His fame, however, had another source: He had dared compete with the locals at their own game.

Rostov sold everything under the sun, but its first and primary product came from its soil, Russia's famed black earth, its chernozem. The city does not fall within the administrative borders of the *Chernozemie*, the Black Earth region that is centered on the Volga city of Voronezh and encompasses the five provinces north and east. Yet on the outskirts of Rostov, one found the same endless fields of rich silt loam that coat the steppes for three thousand miles from Ukraine to Siberia. Black earth is the dark, clumped-together soil that gleams like a black rainbow when its crevices catch the afternoon sun. Born of a thousand years' decomposition of ancient steppe grass, black earth holds no chalk and no dryness. Few soils are richer in nutrients, and fewer hold water better. Black earth is found elsewhere, but no nation has as much as Russia. Like a belt unbuckled across the country's girth, it spans its central regions, coating more than 150 million acres chestnut brown. "The tsar of soils," Vasily Dokuchaev, the nineteenth-century father of Russian earth science, called chernozem. "More valuable than oil," Dokuchaev called the soil, "more precious than gold."

Yet for all its promise, much of the great acreage lies fallow. Russia's black earth, perhaps like no other of its vast natural resources, betrays the burden of the country's abundance, the bequest that somehow seems too much to bear. Rostov, in the heart of the Russian breadbasket, seemed to carry the weight of its past, even the remote days mournfully evoked in the greatest literary work of medieval Russia. "The black earth beneath the hooves," writes the anonymous author of the twelfth-century epic *The Lay*

19

of Igor's Campaign, "was sown with bones and watered with blood: a harvest of sorrow came up over the land of Russia."

THE CITY HAD LONG been the country's wheat, barley, and grain capital. John Warren, however, had seen something else, sunflowers. For hours on the train the yellow fields lit the cabin. In the endless stretches of gold, the tall plants stretched toward the sun, their faces black with seeds. Kolya spoke lovingly, almost romantically, of the seeds. It was a ballad sung across the country. Russians love their *semechki*. Every city, town, and village, no matter how small, was sure to have the seeds on sale–in the markets, at the bus stops, on the streets, and in the passageways below. Black bread and white water remained the first loves. But in the post-Soviet era sunflower seeds became the staple one could be sure to find no matter how bleak the outpost.

Seeds, Warren had to admit, were not gold. But they held oil. Rostov sunflower oil, he thought, could be shipped across the Black Sea and sold in Europe. Business had been good. Now forty-two employees helped him broker everything the black earth had to offer: grains, barley, hops, nuts. *Angliisky khleborob*, they called him in town, the "English peasant." He and his family enjoyed an enormous apartment, a floor above the local governor's. It'd been no fun, of course, to resettle the herd of eighteen who'd lived in it as a *kommunalka*. But the place really had a glow now. Tsarist antiques filled its elegant rooms, while gilt-framed canvases–"fabulous fakes," Warren boasted, of nineteenth-century oils–crowded its walls. Not long ago he'd bought a cigarette boat in Istanbul and motored home–"eight sublime days"–across the Black Sea and up the Don.

That evening I'd caught a report on the news that a worthy in local business had been killed. The deceased had resided, Warren explained, directly below. The apartment, now vacated, seemed a natural target for annexation. "Not a chance," he said. "Everyone would think I whacked him for it."

We went for a meal on Rostov's Left Bank, arriving at a line of tiered restaurants so gaudy with neon they resembled casinos. One was even called Vegas. En route, at the entrance of a dirt road running deep into a tall field of steppe grass, we passed a sign that read CHANCE. "Open-air bordello," Warren explained.

He pulled the Defender into Boris's Place and we were given the center table on the patio. Warren promptly requested a new waitress–Natasha was his favorite–and ordered deep bowls of sickly crawfish and shashlik sizzling in fat. He'd asked me to join him. English visitors were in town. They needed tending. "EBRD gents," he said, contract consultants from the European Bank for Reconstruction and Development. He feared boredom looming and intended to stave it off.

No sooner had Natasha lavished us with food and drink than the lights began to flash, the music blared, and a quartet of dancing girls sidled up. They wore pastel veils, red halter tops, loose trousers of gauzy white. To the electrified beat of "Hava Nagila," the Gypsies began to gyrate. The EBRD gents were overwhelmed. The younger of the two, newly married, tried to bury his head in his crawfish. His partner, however, a gray-haired economist recently retired and eager "to help out the poor Russians," forgot about food. Warren whooped and clapped and stuffed hundred-ruble notes into spandex straps.

"From all of us," he shouted.

"No, allow me!" cried the elder economist, tucking his own rubles into the elastic wiggling beside him.

Our host, Boris, stopped by. It was not his real name. Like most of the men who ran the clubs of the Left Bank, Boris was Armenian. Would we desire company? he wondered, nodding toward a table of gaunt girls in a corner. They wore black and looked bored. No, we were fine, Warren said. Before long the table of girls merged with a table of men next to us. They were a grim crew, anchored by two large pockmarked gentlemen. One wore a white suit, the other black. They both bore gold chains and bracelets. Kingpins from the local Azeri and Georgian mobs, Warren explained. "Colleagues and competitors." Didn't he ever worry about safety? "No," said the honorary consul. "We've got a simple arrangement. I control twelve percent of the market. That's my limit. Anything more, I'm dead."

FOUR

THE TALE READ AS IF it had been lifted from Gogol. It was just one of hundreds, testimonials collected in a book hanging in the half-light of the dank entranceway on Lermontov Street.

My boy went missing back in January '95, when his tank burned in Grozny. Write down his name: Aleshkin, Kostya. Went in when he was nineteen. From the Orenburg region, station Donguzskaya. They only told me in the spring that he'd gone missing. I went to Chechnya, found his commanders. They were kind, didn't kick me out. They fed me and told me to go home, that my Kostya was not among their dead and not among their wounded. So I went to the Chechen fighters. They didn't insult me either; they swore to their Allah that my Kostya wasn't among their prisoners. Then someone said: "Go to Rostov; that's where the unknown are kept in refrigerator train cars." I only came now. I wasn't up to it before and I had no hope. Here I met a young doctor, Borya. He took me to the train car. It was all corpses, some without heads, some without arms, others without legs. I looked through them—but my Kostya wasn't there. I went to bed, and just as I fell asleep I saw Kostya. He said, "Mama, how could you walk past me? Come back tomorrow. I'm lying in the first row, third from the end. Only I've got no face. It burned off. But there's still that birthmark under my arm. You remember." The next day I went to the train car and found Kostya straightaway—just where he said he was.

Chekhov in his diary wrote, "Alas, what is terrible is not the skeletons, but the fact that I am no longer terrified of them." The words raised a bitter smile on the lips of Vladimir Vladimirovich Shcherbakov. He was a military doctor, the head of Military-Medical Laboratory No. 124, known more precisely among the women who traveled to it from all corners of the country as a morgue. Rostov was not just a city of trade. It had a second life as an army town, the military headquarters for the North Caucasus. Its cafés were filled with camouflage, and its streets with UAZik jeeps. Lying, as a matter of considerable convenience, nearly halfway between Moscow and Grozny, the city also served as the main repository of the dead from Chechnya. Since 1995 Shcherbakov and his team of forensic sleuths had tried to return Russia's dead sons to their mothers. When I walked into his morgue, more than three hundred unidentified corpses remained locked in its refrigerated recesses. Two hundred and seventy had been there since the first Chechen war.

Tall and thin, Shcherbakov coiled his long legs behind a big desk piled with red files. He wore thick glasses and a yellow sleeveless shirt with three gold stars on its epaulets. A double-headed eagle adorned a tie clip that held a short blue tie tight against his frame. The office was small, spare. Over his shoulder hung a faded poster of the Virgin Mary in repose. For years now the women of the Soldiers Mothers' Committee had tirelessly dispatched mothers to his door. He had never tried to dissuade them. "What can I do," he said, "but let them search?" The mothers, in turn, called him the Good Doctor.

The morgue took them all, but the dead who remained, the doctor explained, were "the most severe contingent"—those impossible to identify visually. In contrast with the U.S. Army, the Russian military sent its soldiers into war without keeping fingerprints, let alone dental histories and DNA samples. The sleuths were lucky to get ID mug shots. In a room down the hall a balding man in a white lab coat peered into a computer, his eyes only inches from the screen. The monitor was filled with smudge lines, the inked tips of a man's fingers. The technician, Valery Rakitin, had just inked the prints from the corpse. "Wasn't much left," he said. The dogs had made a mess. "Only four fingers and a couple of toes."

The soldier had died at twenty-two. His mother, a forty-four-year-old teacher from Kemerevo, a coal-mining city in Siberia, had called that morning. She had come to collect him. In another age, a decade earlier, I'd been in Kemerevo. Lera, my friend who'd hosted me with her husband, Andrei, in their *kommunalka* in Moscow, came from there. In those days Kemerovo was synonymous with worker unrest; the miners had been among the first to strike as Soviet power ebbed. The boy who had died in Chechnya, been abandoned to the strays, and lain for months unidentified had left a hometown cold and bleak, a blighted city shorn of Siberia's beauty long before his birth.

On the screen, Valery compared the squiggles of a right palm with the whorls of a right forefinger. "Not perfect," he said. But the odds were "extremely good" it was the young man from Kemerevo. He pointed to the prints. "Almost identical," he said. "A match at a degree of one in a thousand." I got the idea—comparing prints and weighing the frequency of like patterns—but the calculus was beyond me. A local programmer had designed the software that tallied the probabilities pertaining to every known fingerprint pattern. Probables were matched, and the composite comparison yielded a percent range for positive identification. The system was far from perfect, Valery conceded, but it gave a fair estimate. Short of genetic analysis, it was the best the state could afford.

Across the narrow room sat Valery's wife. Svetlana had no computer on her desk, only a small white candle that stood before an icon framed in aluminum. "Valery takes care of the boys," she said, "and I take care of the mothers." She lit the candle. The mother from Siberia would be here soon.

NEARLY FIFTY, Shcherbakov could have retired. He was a local, born in the Don village of Aksai. He'd studied in Petersburg, then Leningrad, at the prestigious military medical academy there. Then it was the navy–Pacific Fleet destroyers, tours from Mozambique to Vietnam. His wife, Zina, worked at his side. She was his head nurse. They'd met over an operating table. Their daughter, Yelena, was in medical school, and their son, Andrei, fourteen, was heading for the military academy. Shcherbakov could have been enjoying the quiet at home. Theirs was a small house; an apple orchard lined the creek out back. But he couldn't quit. Returning an identity to the dead was more than a duty. It had become a calling.

There was nothing dramatic, Shcherbakov said, nothing unusual or heroic in the work, nothing that deserved any sympathy. Orthodoxy, he said, did not allow it. Everyone, he was certain, was given his own cross according to his abilities and had to carry it with dignity. At times, when he could deliver a mother and a father from uncertainty, a sense of relief did come. For the parents, he said, not knowing was worse than knowing. "If they can leave here with certainty, they can go home, defeat their grief, and find peace."

Down the hall the mother from Siberia had arrived. The fingerprints remained enlarged on the computer. She sat with her back to the burning candle and stared at the screen. "There you see it," the technician said. He leaned back in his chair.

The mother called him Doctor—in deference to the white lab coat—but was not convinced. "I see absolutely nothing," she said. She rubbed her eyes with a yellow handkerchief in tight, furious circles. "I see nothing," she said again. "But if you say they're his, I believe you. I do. I must. What else can I do?"

FIVE

ROSTOV HAD ITS pleasures, but the hotel was not among them. The phone rang incessantly each night–always females, always the same question: *"You need girl now?"*–before I pulled the plug from the wall. Then they took to knocking on the door. Worse, one morning I got out of bed to discover the sheet blackened with blotches–dozens of dead cockroaches. So when after a week Shvedov flew down from Moscow, I was happy to see him.

He arrived kitted out for battle. He wore Red Army surplus: old khaki jacket and trousers, layered with pockets and liberally frayed. It was Shvedov's idea of camouflage for journalists. He'd also brought the satellite phone I'd rented in Moscow and an old army backpack stuffed with six cartons of *papirosi.* Native to Russia, foul-smelling and absurdly strong, *papirosi* do not even pretend to be cigarettes. Stuffed with rough tobacco, they end not with a filter but with a long, hollow tube of rolled cardboard. Their drag, made famous by Jack London, is so coarse even hardened smokers–Russian, French, Vietnamese–beg off. *Papirosi*, however, have a singular virtue, never lost on Shvedov. They are cheap. A pack runs under five cents.

By then the world had heard of Andrei Babitsky, the Radio Liberty reporter who had dared report from the Chechen side of the war and been arrested by the Russians. Babitsky had suffered a dubious POW "swap," when the FSB staged a videotaped handover, turning the reporter over from its officers to masked men, who were almost certainly FSB operatives. Held captive for months, Babitsky had become a *cause célèbre*.[4] Nobody, however, outside a small circle of Moscow journalists, had ever heard of Shvedov. He did not write much, and he did no radio. But he was one of the best in the business. Born to a father who toiled in the upper reaches of GOSPLAN, the Soviet planning ministry, Shvedov did have a degree in journalism– Moscow State, late 1970s–and a string of credentials–BBC, NTV, *Moscow News*–not all of them false. Given the Kremlin's strict ban on journalists' traveling independently in Chechnya, the robust kidnapping market, and the only other option a government tour in a press herd, I sought out Shvedov.[5] I came to regret it, but he was well recommended. Just as it was hard to imagine Chechnya without war, it was hard to imagine Shvedov without the war in Chechnya. Since Moscow had moved to quash Dudayev's rebellion in 1994, he may have traveled to the region more than any journalist. Oddly, he never called the republic by its name. To him, it was always the Zone.

I had hoped things would get better farther south. I tried to talk Zhenya, the shy Cossack, all elbows and bony arms, who had driven me around Rostov, into delivering us to our next stop, Nalchik, capital of Kabardino-Balkaria. The small republic was sleepy and well within the borders of Russia, but Zhenya hedged. He had long been out of work. His income now derived from his Lada, but his face contorted at the prospect of crossing the city limits. "Down there," he said quietly, "you never know quite where you are."

Zhenya would go only as far as Mineralniye Vody (Mineral Waters), the first of the weary tsarist spa towns that lay a long day's drive to the south. We left Rostov as the car market opened, well before dawn, moving southeast along the Rostov–Baku Highway. The Route 66 of the North Caucasus, the road had once carried Soviet travelers directly through Grozny to the shores of the Caspian. Now, thanks to the years of bombings, assassinations, and war, it was clogged with checkpoints.

As we drove south, the road itself seemed to take a leisurely, southerly dip. All the while, Shvedov smoked without pause and rarely let a moment pass unbroken by commentary. He drove poor Zhenya crazy. He tried the radio but caught only static. Zhenya had mastered the Russian technique, passed down through the generations, of economizing on gas. He would accelerate only to take the car out of gear and coast, repeating the procedure every time the road regained its slope. I sat in the back of the Lada, alone, watching the landscape evolve. Thin stands of willows now ran through the sunflower fields, lining the creeks that rent the earth. Every so often pastures appeared, stretches of green where mottled cows grazed, the fattest I had seen in Russia.

By afternoon we had driven eight hours and crossed into the *krai*, or administrative region, of Stavropol. We had also, even before we saw them, felt the mountains. As we approached Mineralniye Vody, the dark massifs of the Caucasus appeared, giant shadows like clouds against the summer sky. At first the peaks stood stiffly in a tight row. Yet as we drove on, they rose ever higher, each revealing its own grandiose contours. One peak towered-above the others: Elbrus. Too large for Zhenya's cracked windshield to compass, it seemed a castle in the sky, insurmountable and unreal. At 18,510 feet, Elbrus, the two-headed cone of a sleeping volcano, was not only one of the pillars of the Caucasus but also the highest mountain in Europe.

We had reached a fault line. After the green fields and streams, now before us spread the dusty foothills of the mountainous bridge that linked the Black Sea to the west with the Caspian to the east. For centuries the mapmakers have marked the Caucasus as the dividing line between Europe and Asia, Christendom and Islam. Stretching more than six hundred miles, since the Soviet fall the range has separated Russia from the former Soviet states of Georgia, Armenia, and Azerbaijan to the south. The lands north of the massifs, known collectively as the North Caucasus, comprise seven ethnic homelands, some gerrymandered, some legitimate, that fall within the borders of the Russian Federation. In all, the region is a linguistic and ethnic labyrinth, where as many as fifty different peoples speak their own tongues. In the first post-Soviet decade the pot boiled, gaining fame as the Caucasian Cauldron, an impossible corner of the world fated to suffer "ethnic hatreds," "religious divides," and unwanted attention for its oil. Yet as our little Lada chugged on south, taking in the expanse of rock, snow, and ice, I could not help wondering if geology, not geopolitics, still governed these lands.

We drove on, trading Zhenya for Khassan, Cossack for Caucasian, to Pyatigorsk, the Town of Five Mountains, a resort, founded in 1780, where the Good and the Great took the waters. For the aristocracy of nineteenth-century Russia, it was their Baden Baden. In 1841, Lermontov, at twenty-six, died here in a famous duel. The spot in the woods nearby where he fell remained a destination for Russians. The town still offered grand vistas and poplar-lined promenades, but it no longer looked noble, much less restorative. Even on a fine summer day Pyatigorsk looked depopulated and defoliated. The warfare to the east and west had taken a toll. The tourists now stayed away.

By dusk we had reached Nalchik, the inert capital of the tiny republic of Kabardino-Balkaria. We settled into a white-columned sanatorium, an old Soviet retreat among the firs, refashioned by a Turk into a hotel, the Grand Kavkaz. Kabardino-Balkaria was best known as a source of mineral water, mountain horses, and soccer stars. But it was also a prime example of the Bolshevik manipulation of the peoples of the North Caucasus. Kabardino-Balkaria, like its neighbor Karachaevo-Cherkessia, was a Leninist creation.

The genius of Lenin, Ali Kazikhanov, editor of *Severny Kavkaz*, explained, was to throw the Kabardins and Balkars together in one hyphenated republic in 1921, separating them from their natural allies the Cherkess and Karachai. As Kazikhanov told it, the history sounded like a Bolshevik game of checkers, with national destinies at stake. The Kabardins, by far the majority, were related to the Cherkess, while the Balkars shared a Turkic tongue with the Karachai. Each had a separate history, but Moscow entangled them, forcing rivals to share homelands. "It wasn't just 'divide and conquer,'" said Kazikhanov. "It was 'divide, conquer, and tie up in trouble.'"

I remembered Lenin's pushpins. Years earlier I'd driven into the woods outside Moscow to Gorki Leninskie, the estate where Lenin died in 1924, to see a replica of his old Kremlin office, complete with his desk, books, and paperweight—a bronze chimpanzee knitting its brow. (Yeltsin had ordered the original office removed—along with Stalin's—as part of his extravagant renovation of the Kremlin.) One wall of Lenin's study was covered with a map, its southern edges dotted with pins, each a different color. Lenin had kept a close eye on the ethnic and religious labyrinth of the Caucasus.

The Soviet map was drawn to maintain a false balance, the editor Kazikhanov said. Contradictions intended to preoccupy the natives. It was easy for him to explain the history of hatred between the Kabardins and Balkars. He belonged to neither group. He was a Kumyk from Dagestan. And he edited, naturally, a newspaper printed in Russian, the only language common among the peoples.

SIX

FOR THREE LANGUID days in Nalchik, I had to avoid the local president. A Kabardin—his prime minister was a Balkar—he had "requested" that I interview him. With no interest in being drawn into a squabble between Kabardins and Balkars, I decided to abandon both. Outside the Grand Kavkaz, I found Ismail, asleep in an ancient Audi. We struck a deal to head farther south, to travel in the shadows of the mountains to Vladikavkaz, capital of the next small republic on the road to Chechnya, North Ossetia.

With the fat end of his fist Ismail banged the tape I'd pulled from my bag into the Audi's cassette player. And so as we drove on through the operatic scenery, two Russian helicopters now limning the foothills to our right, Eric Clapton accompanied us, singing of tears in heaven. When we reached Vladikavkaz, the sun was a giant ball of burnt orange sinking behind the peak that towered behind the town, Mount Kazbek, another giant of the Caucasus range, on the Georgian side.[6] The streets, to my surprise, were crowded. Only the day before, a bomb had produced havoc in the central market, killing six and wounding forty-three. The remote-controlled device, a police investigator later told me, had been well made, designed to rip as much flesh as possible. We had descended a rung lower into the cauldron. Vladikavkaz, however, had grown inured to bombings. They had become seasonal. The previous spring a bomb had killed sixty-two. "Market squabbles" the locals called the explosions. With Chechnya so close, the North Ossetians affected an easygoing air, a rare commodity in the region and one they were eager to promote.

"Welcome to the oasis," said the president of the republic, Aleksandr Sergeyevich Dzasokhov, gesturing grandly like a cruise ship director as we sat down in his office. It was a long suite of oak-paneled rooms, so long it seemed without end. "Surrounded by war, we live in peace with our neighbors and, most important, with Moscow." Dzasokhov had been a member of Gorbachev's Politburo. Tall and elegantly dressed, he was more than a silver-haired survivor. He was a patrician master of Caucasian deal making. Dzasokhov knew he was only telling half of the truth. He was well aware of the difference between an oasis and a mirage.

Vladikavkaz, christened as a garrison town in 1818, means "To rule the Caucasus." The North Ossetians have yet to live up to the bravado, but they have long served as the proxies of tsars and general secretaries in helping tame the unruly tribes of the south. In August 1942 Hitler's troops planted a Nazi flag atop Elbrus. Hitler wanted the Grozny oil fields and dreamed of taking Baku, with its vast reserves of Caspian oil.[7] Not surprisingly, in some Caucasian circles, the Germans found support.[8] How many sided with the Nazis is a matter of historical debate. No one will ever know. To some, the Germans doubtless offered a chance to oppose Soviet power. The Ossetians, however, stood loyal. The Nazi forces got no farther than Vladikavkaz, then called Ordzhonikidze after a Georgian aide-de-camp to Stalin.

In recent years North Ossetia had distinguished itself as a singular outpost of fidelity. Things, however, could have gone very differently. In the last years of the old empire, as minor satraps across the south raised the sword of religion and the shield of sovereignty to revive "ancient hatreds" remembered by few, North Ossetia was the first Soviet tinderbox to explode. In the late 1980s, tensions boiled between the North Ossetians and the Ingush, the ethnic minority to the east—and the Chechens' next of kin. Both sides claimed the pastoral land east of Vladikavkaz known as Prigorodny, just on the North Ossetian side of the border with Ingushetia.

The roots of the trouble, like much of the present turmoil, began with Stalin, who in 1944 ordered the Ingush and the Chechens deported en masse to Central Asia. On February 23, 1944, Red Army Day, and the twenty-sixth anniversary of the founding of the workers' and peasants' army, Stalin tricked the Ingush and the Chechens into coming out to their town squares. They were rounded up and packed off—in lend-lease Studebaker trucks.[9] For the next thirteen years, until the liberalizing thaw that followed Khrushchev's secret speech of 1956, when they started to return to the lands, the Chechens and the Ingush disappeared from the pages of officialdom. The Soviet Union had established a tradition, as Robert Conquest notes in his seminal book on the deportations, *The Nation Killers*, of erasing the existence of intellectuals who had earned the wrath of the state. "Unpersons," George Orwell had famously called the writers and poets who were erased from Soviet society, if not killed. But as Conquest points out in regard to Stalin's rounding up of the Chechens and Ingush, among other minorities, "the 'unnation' was a new phenomenon."[10]

Before the deportation Prigorodny was Ingush. In the last years of the USSR the Ingush began to exhibit their intention of reclaiming it. In 1992, their Soviet bonds loosened, the Ingush and the North Ossetians went to war over the scrap of land. The fighting cost hundreds of lives on both sides, but the North Ossetians, backed by Moscow, kept their hold on the dry pastures of Prigorodny.

There had been another small war, across the mountains in Georgia, beyond the famed Darial Pass, among the Ossetians trapped in another contrivance of Soviet mapmaking called South Ossetia. In 1989 the South Ossetians, with a population of some ninety thousand, had risen up, seeking to break free of Georgia and reunite with their brethren to the north. No

nation on earth, however, recognized their sovereignty.[11] The North Ossetians meanwhile remained loyal to Moscow. Fealty had its rewards. The tiny
republic of fewer than a half million now led the Russian Federation in
vodka production. "Ours is a special relationship," President Dzasokhov said
of the coziness with the Russians. "We have a history of understanding."

In Moscow the North Ossetians had long been seen as kindred Orthodox amid the sea of Muslims, yet they led a double life. The first clue came
outside the president's office: an oil painting depicting a white-bearded warrior charging through the air on a white stallion. "A local hero" the president
had called him. "Our own St. George." The second clue came on a winding
road through the mountains. Rusik, a proud native of Vladikavkaz and an
old friend of Shvedov's, was doing his best to keep us on the road, its edges
fast giving way to the craggy scarps. He was once a KGB major but in the
spirit of the times had reincarnated himself. Rusik had made an enterprise
out of the town's aspiring entrepreneurs. He headed the new Small Business
Association. The group was "still growing," he conceded. There was plenty
of downtime. When I asked about Dargavs, known as the Village of the
Dead, he'd reached for the keys to his jeep.

The village lay high in the mountains a hundred turns above
Vladikavkaz. On a terraced hillside in a steep green valley dotted purple and
red with wildflowers, the tombs at first looked like giant beehives. But when
we neared, they came into focus as tapered mounds of slate stacked tight.
The oldest tombs dated from the thirteenth century. Each was a family sep-
ulcher, a resting place open to the mountain breeze and, bizarrely, the eyes
of strangers. Peering into the half-light of the shrines, one could not miss the
skeletons of generations of sheep farmers. Stretched out atop one another,
they lay as straight as they had been put to rest. In the shadows, skin, yellow
and thick like burlap, gave glow to the bones.

The balance of the sun, mountain air, and crossing winds, Rusik heard,
was perfect here. It had preserved the dead. The Russian guidebooks and
the villagers below claimed the tradition had long ago yielded to Soviet
secularism. Rusik, however, led me in silence farther up the hill, to a female
corpse. "Look closely," he said, "and judge for yourself." I could see fabric
wrapped around the bones. It was machine-woven, a skirt of faded cotton. The Ossetians, it seemed, had maintained the practice well into the
modern era.

Arguably the most Russified of the peoples of the North Caucasus, the Ossetians claimed ancient roots. They were the modern heirs of the Sarmatians, Indo-Iranian sun-worshipers who had pushed the Scythians from the southern steppes by the second century B.C. While their neighbors spoke tongues native to the Caucasus or Turkic languages, Ossetian derived from Persian. North Ossetia had even rechristened itself Alania, after the Alans, a Sarmatian tribe.

Officialdom may have wished to deny it, but the locals remained devout in the old ways. Outside Vladikavkaz I visited Hetag's Grove, a sacred stand of giant trees amid brown fields where Ossetians bowed before an ancient god named Wasterzhi.[12] I spent a morning in the wood toasting the god with homemade fire brew in the company of three Ossetian soldiers on home leave from Chechnya—and desirous of deliverance. Shvedov dismissed the idea of any local paganism from the start. "Ossetians are Christian," he insisted, "as Orthodox as Russians." Rusik, however, kept silent. It was not right, he said, catching my eyes in the jeep's mirror, to talk of such things.

SEVEN

WE MADE IT TO NAZRAN, the would-be capital of the would-be statelet of Ingushetia, in time for lunch. Rusik arranged for Soslan, the Small Business Association's driver, to take us. We drove slowly through the eerie silence of the old Prigorodny battleground—its houses burned out, its fields still fallow—before coming to the border with Ingushetia. Soslan, of course, being Ossetian, could go no farther. Shvedov and I walked across the dirt road to the border post, a hut, and, after haggling for an hour with the Ingush guards, entered the last little republic in the foothills of the Caucasus before Chechnya.

Nazran in the Soviet era was a market town, a dusty assemblage of collective farms that raised cattle and sheep and little else. When in the late 1950s the Ingush and the Chechens returned from their Central Asian exile, they resettled in a single administrative province, first established by Moscow in 1934 and generously named the Chechen-Ingush Autonomous

Republic. In 1991, when the Chechens unilaterally opted to end the curse of their hyphenated past, Ingushetia was born by default. Like any fledgling state, it soon gained a president: Ruslan Aushev, a homegrown general and a mustachioed hero of the Soviet war in Afghanistan. Naturally, a president required a seat of power.

Shvedov had dreaded Nazran. There was only one place, he'd said, that scared him more than the Zone, Ingushetia. He'd said it again and again. In Nazran, he'd warned, the price on my head doubled, and his confidence in the authorities vanished. The fighting remained across the border, but the war had seeped everywhere into Ingush life. Nazran was a breeding ground for kidnappers, assassins, bombers. It was also, as a result of a 1994 quid pro quo with the Kremlin, an *ofshornaya zona*, a new term in post-Soviet jurisprudence that denoted a realm known in the West as an offshore tax haven.[13] Everywhere the red-brick palazzi, as big as any in the woods outside Moscow, testified to the local growth industries in bootleg vodka, petroleum products, and arms. The Ingush hated to say it, and few did, but the war in Chechnya had been good to them.

The Ingush and Chechens speak closely related tongues. Brothers in the Vainakh nation–the word means "our people"–they share many cultural and religious traditions. But the years of war had strained the fraternity. Never ones to fight in the Chechens' defense, by now the Ingush had turned hostile. In the first campaign they had taken in Chechen refugees. But in the second round, Chechens had flooded across the border. As the storming of Grozny loomed, nearly two hundred thousand Chechen refugees had fled to Ingushetia, nearly doubling the tiny republic's population.

Outside Nazran we found two dozen Chechen families living in an abandoned pigsty. Shvedov found the irony–Muslims sleeping beside pig troughs–amusing. The camps farther on, however, left even him speechless. Here, for miles on the parched earth, thousands of Chechen refugees were trying to live. They were eating, sleeping, and, on a rare occasion, washing in a city of tents, the likes of which the world saw with regularity now, thanks to CNN and the end of the post–cold war bliss. At the height of the second Chechen war, the Sputnik and Karabulak camps had housed tens of thousands. Six thousand remained.

It was a stifling summer day. In the tents, skin streamed with sweat. The train cars were even worse, much worse. The old Soviet cars, four dozen in all, had been dragged to the edge of the barren field and left to stand in place. There was no breeze and no water, nothing but flies and a rising rate of infection. For 3,657 Chechens, the train was home. The men squatted in the shade of the carriages and watched the day go by. Their wives said they had ceased to be men. There was no work and no money. How could they be men? The women offered dry crackers and black tea. Had it been "back then," they said, had we been "over there," they could have hosted me properly. Not all them knew, but nearly all suspected, that the homes they had left behind were no longer.

The talk came to a end when the water truck arrived. The water came from the canal, two miles away. In an hour another truck came. Bread. There was no water here, the women explained. And no flour. There were only children. Everywhere, in the dirt, by the outhouses, under the train cars stopped in their tracks, the children played. So there would be a future, the women said, but what kind?

IF VLADIKAVKAZ BREATHED with the mystique of the nineteenth-century Caucasus, Nazran still lived by Soviet deal making. Whatever it was you wanted—a bottle of beer or a rack of lamb, an interview with the president or a ride to the camps—it was always negotiated through a side door, in the back of the shop, under the table. The epicenter of the negotiations was the Hotel Assa. A place of legend, the Assa was built in the euphoric first years after the Soviet fall as a Western-style hotel and business center, the first to grace this side of the Caucasus. Given the bloodshed and misery a few miles away, the Ingush investment climate had failed to lure many prospectors. The Assa instead since its first days had played host, and faithfully hustled, the journalists and relief workers drawn to the war. On a good day the foreigners nearly outnumbered the agents of the Ingush arm of the Federal Security Service, the FSB. The hotel claimed three stars and possessed, at first glance, the reassuring appearance of a tidy refuge from the dust, an outpost of modernity, if not air-conditioning.

Shvedov had looked forward to the Assa. For days it had been all he could talk of: the balcony one could eat on, the little artificial lake it overlooked, the presidential town houses across the way, the sweet waitresses he knew by name. His dreams all came true. Within a day he was dictating, in a painful recitation of no less than ten minutes' duration, his four-course meals without a menu. At the Assa we stopped dining together.

It was not hard to see why the hotel had earned a reputation as a hell-hole. The Assa had taken a beating. Hotels in the West often offer lists of local restaurants and recommended boutiques. At the Assa, rooms came with price lists—each item and what it would cost if destroyed: "Broken door: $200. Broken window: $200. Broken bed: $300. Broken shower stall: $400. Broken mirror: $200." The inventory closed with the administration's sincere wish that its guests enjoy a pleasant stay.

The place at least had color. The restaurant each night filled with Belgian doctors, Danish food distributors, even a crew of Irish clowns in from Bosnia to entertain the children in the camps. There was also a German engineer, a veteran relief worker who'd struck out on his own. Over coffee in the morning and drinks at night, he sat on the balcony, mumbling urgently about the *verdammte Chlor*, the damned chlorine. He was gripped by an obsession with the cisterns of chlorine gas in Grozny. I had heard of the cisterns, leftovers from an old Soviet plant. The Russians had claimed the Chechens had blown them up, in an improvised attempt at chemical warfare. The Chechens in turn blamed the Russians for shelling the gas tanks. Now here was the German insisting all the cisterns had not been blown up.

"*Sie sind tam!*" he cried, blending German with Russian. They are there! "*Sie sind* in very bad shape, *diese* tanks! They could explode any day, today, yesterday, *Morgen*. When they do, they kill any brave Chechens who make it *nach Hause.*"

The German failed, it seemed, to recognize that I spoke English. But he was passionate about preventing the chlorine cisterns from exploding. He had a simple plan. He would cool the gas, liquefy it, and store it in trucks while the cisterns were repaired. He figured he needed only a few thousand dollars, but no relief organization would help him. They all ran, he said, at the word "Chechnya." And so the poor German had been left stranded at the Assa. Each night he retreated to the balcony on his own, to drink his furies away.

IN THE REFUGEE CAMPS I had sat in a stifling tent drinking strong tea from glass cups with Kuri Idrisov. He was a rarity, a Chechen psychiatrist. In the first war, he'd worked with a syringe, administering morphine day and night. The hospital in Grozny had been destroyed–twice. In the interregnum, now in his forties, he had joined the French crew of *Médécins du Monde*. For more than a year he had tended to the refugees. His family had moved back to Grozny, to his native village of Aldy, the destination I'd marked on the map I carried every day. The psychiatrist had heard of what happened in Aldy. His relatives had been in the village that day. He had wanted to return with his family, but he said he could not leave. He was hoping to salve the psychic wounds of the children in the tent city.

In another tent the children were listening to Musa Akhmadov. Akhmadov had written a series of books on the Chechens' customary law, the traditions that governed relations among children and elders, lovers and enemies, known as *adat*. The psychiatrist had recruited the writer to spend time with the children. *Adat*, Akhmadov explained, had suffered in the war. It was not a religious but a social code. "The backbone of Chechen culture" he called it. Since the Chechens' earliest days, *adat* had drawn the lines between right and wrong. But in the turmoil of the years of war, a new code–*Shari'a*–the Islamic religious law imported by young men with beards who called themselves Wahhabis had threatened the continuum of *adat*. Wahhabism, a strict form of fundamentalist Islam that originated in Saudi Arabia, had been carried to Chechnya from the Arab diaspora.[14] The two were incompatible, Akhmadov said. He feared that the youngest refugees, with no knowledge of the laws of old, would fall prey to the Wahhabis. The children, the writer worried, would lose their Chechen heritage in the tents.

As we walked outside, threading among the children, Idrisov did not smile. After the first war he had believed it was the Chechens' fault. "We'd won our freedom," he said, "but hadn't learned how to use it." Now he thought differently. This new round had convinced him. "Look around you," he said. "The Russians don't want our land or our oil or our mountains. They want us to die out."

DESPITE SHVEDOV'S HOURLY assurances, Issa had yet to appear in Nazran. For days we called Moscow, trying to relay a message to him in Chechnya. Shvedov, for some reason, insisted on code. "The package," he screamed into the satellite phone, "has arrived and is waiting." Issa turned up at last, claiming car trouble and the backup at the checkpoints from

Grozny. We'd come back late to the Assa when I noticed a large man sitting at a pink plastic table beside the hotel. He was trying to crack pistachios with his fist on the plastic. Shvedov had walked right past him. The man, without looking up from his pursuit, had whistled. Shvedov, fearful the kitchen would close, kept walking. The man called out: "Is that any way to say hello?"

Issa had come to me with the résumé of an opportunist loyal to Moscow. Colleagues he had previously ferried had passed on the collective intelligence: Issa was once a high-ranking official in the anti-Dudayev camp, a staunchly pro-Russian Chechen of the Soviet era. He could be trusted to get you into Chechnya and around the republic–to almost any place no journalist could otherwise get to. But he could not be trusted in any other respect. Rumor cast him as an intermediary in the kidnapping trade.

He looked at me directly, the barest of smiles curling the edges of a thin gray mustache. "My dear Andrei," he said, "I wish you a pleasant stay in the land the world has forgotten."

I don't know what it was. Maybe it was the singing. (He was fond of Joe Dassin, the bards of the Soviet underground, and old Chechen ballads sung, naturally, in Russian.) Maybe it was the way he affected a wordly air. (He mixed, in a single sentence, the few words he knew in French with the few he knew in English.) Maybe it was his gentlemanly manner. (He wore a pressed shirt, a sleeveless undershirt, and polished shoes.) But against my better judgment, Shvedov's insistent counsel, and all that I had heard, I took an immediate liking to Issa.

It was too dark to set out. Issa, however, did not want to stay in the hotel. He knew it was infested with Ingush security agents, men who had no desire to see him working with an American journalist. We would leave before dawn the next day. This time Shvedov was right: It was best not to let Issa out of our sight. The Assa was short on comfort, but it was long on protection. Each night we ate in the restaurant beside men wearing camouflage bodysuits, their Kalashnikovs slung over their chairs. They were the bodyguards of aid workers. Each night there was gunfire outside, but inside, it was quiet. Until our last night.

It was around ten in the evening. I was alone in my room when I was startled by pounding on the door. I opened it and saw only an ID card shoved in my face and a trio of well-armed men in plain clothes. Two had automatic rifles in their hands. The third, a pale fellow dressed all in black who now refused to show me his ID again, wore two holstered guns, one under an armpit, another in his waist. They said they were police, but I knew they were Ingush FSB.

"You have failed to register with the police," the lead man said when I showed him my documents. The hotel should have done that, I said. Like all hotels in Russia, it was required to do so. I had given the clerk my passport and visa. "You've committed a crime," he said. It was a bluff, and one poorly orchestrated. All the same the next hour consisted of a spectacle of pounding on doors, rousting aid workers, and seizing passports. It dragged on to midnight.

In the lobby I found an Austrian relief worker screaming at the Ingush FSB agents. He was pleading for his passport. He knew no Russian, had just arrived, and was justifiably confused. He had come from Vienna to build latrines in the refugee camps. I intervened to tell him that the gentlemen said he could retrieve his passport tomorrow. Did he know where the Interior Ministry was? Of course he did, he cried. His bodyguards worked there.

All the while, the agents of the Ingush secret police spoke of arrests, jail, court orders. In time, however, the threats eased. They spoke of "fines" and then of "exemptions." Before long they simply handed my documents back– with apologies. The lead man in black even offered to buy me a drink. I took a whiskey, a double. Later, once the men had vanished into the starless night just as suddenly as they'd arrived, the relief workers huddled in outrage in the lobby.

What relief organization did I represent? they wanted to know. They were relieved, oddly, to learn I was a journalist. "That explains it," said a Belgian nurse, a longtime Assa resident. The Ingush agents, she said, hadn't given them so much attention for months. Moreover, this time they hadn't really seemed to be after bribes. My presence, the nurse said, explained the goon squad's interest. She had a thought: "You're not going into Chechnya tomorrow, are you?"

EIGHT

THE POISONED EMOTIONS that pervade relations between Russians and Chechens have ample literary precedent. Lermontov's "Cossack Lullaby" is still sung to Russian children at bedtime:

> *Over the rocks the Terek streams*
> *Raising a muddy wave,*
> *Onto the bank the wicked Chechen crawls,*
> *sharpening his dagger as he goes;*
> *But your father is an old warrior,*
> *Forged in many a battle,*
> *So sleep little one, be calm . . .*

For Russia's "people of color" there is no political correctness, no cultural police to purge Russian literature of its jingoism. Russian writers have long coveted, and feared, the Caucasus. Although slurs emerged—Lermontov's "wicked Chechen" is only the most famous—the Chechens were not always cast as bloodthirsty bandits. Pushkin, in his 1822 classic "The Prisoner of the Caucasus," used the south as a lusty backdrop to probe the nature of freedom. To the poet, the Chechens were noble savages who enjoyed a "Circassian liberty" he could only envy. Lermontov, ironically, was no defender of Russian hegemony. In an early poem, "Izmail-Bey," he even undermined the imperial campaign to subdue the mountaineers.[15] Still, by the middle of the nineteenth century, as the Caucasian wars raged, a singular image of the Chechens had formed in the Russian imagination. They were merciless thieves, head choppers who would slit their own mothers' throats should a blood feud demand it. Worse, they lived by taking Russians hostage and holding them in a *zindan*—a dark pit carved into the earth.

If the Russians had poets and writers to blame for their bias, the Chechens owed their opinion of the Russians in large part to one man, General Aleksei Petrovich Yermolov. Under Alexander I and Nicholas I, from 1816 to 1827, Yermolov served as viceroy of the Caucasus, the prime mover of the effort to pacify the mountaineers. In the post-Soviet decade, as the Chechens again acted on their yearning for sovereignty, the old bigotry rose anew in Moscow and across Russia. So, too, as Yeltsin's failed campaign gave way to Putin's new and improved offensive, did the tsarist military strategy. Yermolov was the progenitor of the Russian notion that there was only one way to defeat the Chechens: burn all their villages to the ground. Early in the second Chechen war one of Putin's field marshals struck an uncanny echo of Yermolov's conviction. "Our strategy is simple," General Gennadi Troshev said. "If they shoot at us from a house, we destroy the house. If they shoot from all over a village, we destroy the village."[16]

Yermolov boasted an illustrious résumé even before he reached the Caucasus. A giant of a man—"the head of a tiger on the torso of a Hercules" is how Pushkin portrayed him after an audience in 1829—Yermolov had won the Cross of St. George for heroism in battle when he was sixteen.[17] At the fall of Paris in 1814 he had led both the Russian and Prussian Guards. With the deaths of Kutuzov and Bagration, Yermolov became the most revered officer in the imperial corps.[18] His cruelty was famed. "I desire that the terror of my name should guard our frontiers," he is said to have declared, "that my word should be for the natives a law more inevitable than death. Condescension in the eyes of Asiatics is a sign of weakness, and out of pure humanity I am inexorably severe. One execution saves hundreds of Russians from destruction, and thousands of Mussulmans from treason."[19] By his career's end he had become a legend. "Nothing has any influence on Yermolov," wrote the head of Nicholas's secret police, "except his own vanity."[20]

In short order, Yermolov set out to subdue the south. He built a line of fortresses along the Sunzha River. Forward bases in enemy territory, they bore names declaring his intentions: Groznaya (Menacing) was founded in 1818, the same year as Vladikavkaz, followed by Burnaya (Stormy) and Vnezapnaya (Sudden). He wrote Alexander I, Napoleon's most unyielding foe:

When the fortresses are ready, I shall offer the scoundrels dwelling between the Terek and the Soundja [Sunzha] and calling themselves "peaceable," rules of life, and certain obligations, that will make clear to them that they are subjects of your Majesty, and not allies, as they have hitherto dreamed. If they submit, as they ought, I will apportion them according to their numbers the necessary amount of land . . . if not, I shall propose to them to retire and join the other robbers from whom they differ only in name, and in this case the whole of the land will be at our disposal.[21]

It was psyops, tsarist style. Fortress Groznaya presaged not only the terror to come but the Russians' misguided strategy as well. Yermolov succeeded only in uniting the Chechens and their neighbors to the east, the Dagestanis, in a rebellion led by Imam Shamil, the fabled nineteenth-century Muslim warrior. Shamil's holy war, the *Ghazavat*, lasted more than twenty-five years. As early as 1820 one wise contemporary of Yermolov's foretold his failure. "It is just as hard to subjugate the Chechens and other peoples of this region as to level the Caucasian range," wrote General Mikhail Orlov, who did not fight in the campaign. "This is not something to achieve with bayonets but rather with time and enlightenment, in such short supply in our country. The fighting may bring great personal benefits to Yermolov, but none whatsoever to Russia."[22] In 1859, surrounded by imperial troops, Shamil gave up. But as the Russians knew well, the surrender was tactical. His *Ghazavat* would live on.

WE ARRIVED IN GUDERMES, Chechnya's second–largest city, as the sun set, moments before the shoot-on-sight curfew fell. Chechnya is only slightly larger than the state of Connecticut, covering some six thousand square miles. Once it took a couple of hours to drive from Nazran to Gudermes, the town that rose only a few concrete floors off the dry ground to the north and east of Grozny. Now thanks to the vagaries of the checkpoints and the Russian convoys on the road—the endless caravans of tanks, trucks, and kerchiefed soldiers clinging atop armored personnel carriers (APCs)—it took us the whole day. Gudermes had little to offer. But the Russians, in an attempt to lend a semblance of governance to their military adventure had made it the republic's temporary capital. Grozny was in no shape to host the officers and bureaucrats visiting from Moscow.

Issa, exhausted, went to his bedroom to undress. He rolled a small rug across the uneven floor and, stripped down to his sleeveless T-shirt and undershorts, bent to his knees to pray. Shvedov meanwhile was overjoyed. "Not a bad day's work," he said, declaring it over, as one shoe removed the other. He pulled off a sweat-soaked shirt, lay across an old sofa, and reached for another *papirosa* cigarette. As he smoked, the sweat continued to drip from his bald head.

It had been a long day. We'd started out early in the morning, crossed into Chechnya, driven across its dry northern plains and into the remains of Grozny. I had seen Kabul in the summer of 1996, just before the Taliban took the Afghan capital. Leveled so many times, Kabul had no cityscape. Little, save the remnants of the old Soviet apartment blocks, distinguished it from the Stone Age. Grozny, however, looked worse, much worse. When the USSR collapsed, the Chechen capital had been a modern city of Soviet architecture and European aspirations. It had been a city with promenades and parks, where the sweet smell of jasmine mingled with the smell of grilling lamb at sidewalk stands, where mammoth industrial works—one of the USSR's largest petroleum refineries, a chemical factory, a cement plant—belched black plumes day and night, ever reminding the residents of their service to the empire. The square blocks downtown had once boasted the landmarks of Soviet power—Party buildings of stone that lengthened the reach of the ministries in Moscow. Grozny had once been a destination for the ambitious from across the North Caucasus, a center of education (with a university, technical institutes, sixty schools) and culture (with a national library, fine arts museum, museum of national culture, puppet theater, drama theater, and concert hall).

There had also been people. Grozny before the first war was home to nearly half a million residents. Between Lenin Square and Lenin Park, university students had gathered in the long summer evenings at the square named in honor of the *druzhba narodov* ("friendship of peoples"). Nearby stood a famous statue that pretended to testify to the ethnic solidarity. Three Bolsheviks—a Chechen, an Ingush, and a Russian—were sculpted in stone, shoulder to shoulder. The years of war, however, had laid the myth bare. The heads of the happy trio had been blown off by a rocket-propelled grenade.[23] Now everything was different. Nothing functioned, and little remained. Grozny was a city of ruins.

We entered the long Staropromyslovsky district. Block after block had been bombed and burned out. Of the few buildings that still stood, many were sliced open. Walls and roofs had fallen, revealing the abandoned remains of homes inside: sinks, burned cabinets, old stoves. Furniture, belongings, anything of value had disappeared long ago. We drove on, accelerating between the checkpoints, now approaching the city center. Each turn revealed only more concrete carcasses, more black metal twisted and torched, more gaping holes that held only darkness. "This," announced Issa, though the images required no captions, "is the wreckage of Putin's War."

FOR THE CHECHENS the winter of 1999–2000 may have been the harshest ever. While the West greeted the new millennium with apprehension, fearful that computers and fiber optics might usher in the Apocalypse, Armageddon had already arrived for the Chechens. The fortunate ones had survived one horrible war, the campaign that began on New Year's Eve 1994 and ended for all practical purposes on August 6, 1996, the day the Chechen fighters swarmed back and retook Grozny. The first war left as many as one hundred thousand dead. Launched to quell a nationalist movement for independence, it dragged on thanks largely to Yeltsin's vanity, the shambolic state of his armed forces, and the resolve of the Chechen rebels. In the summer of 1996 Yeltsin won reelection, and "the Chechen question" was put on hold. On August 31, 1996, Yeltsin's envoy, General Aleksandr Lebed, cut a deal with Aslan Maskhadov, the shy military leader of the insurgency.[24] The pact, signed in the Dagestani town of Khasavyurt, brought a cease-fire but put off the critical issue of the region's status for five years. The deal haunted both sides. "Khasavyurt," in the coded lexicon of Moscow politics, lingered as a metaphor for Russia's weakness.

David had beaten Goliath but not killed him. The rewards were few. For Chechens the interregnum brought an ugly period of isolation, dominated by banditry, kidnapping, and arbitrary attempts at *Shari'a*. In January 1997 Maskhadov was elected the first Chechen president, but even he had no illusions the republic had attained sovereignty or peace.[25] In Moscow, Chechnya was pushed to the back burner, its troubles relegated to the expanding realm of the country's political taboos, another embarrassment best left unspoken and forgotten.

Then, one warm morning in August 1999, the back burner caught fire. The two most famous fighters of the first war, Shamil Basayev and the Saudi-born mercenary known as Khattab (his single *nom de guerre*), opened a new front. The Kremlin had made Basayev Russia's most wanted man after he had led a daring, and homicidal, raid on a hospital in the southern Russian town of Budyonnovsk in the summer of 1995. Basayev had led the rebels' return to Grozny on August 6, 1996, but struggled after the war. For a time he tried governing, serving briefly as prime minister under Maskhadov. By his own admission, Basayev as a politician was a disaster. His talent lay in warfare. Khattab, meanwhile, had become the most odious rebel to the Russians. An Islamic militant with a sinister giggle and long, curly hair, on Russian television he was branded the Black Arab. Khattab had joined the Chechen fight in 1995, having fought the Soviets in Afghanistan. In Afghanistan, by his own admission, Khattab had consorted with Osama bin Laden. But the rebel commander's ties to bin Laden were obscure at best.[26]

Basayev and Khattab led a convoy of fighters across the mountains of southeastern Chechnya, east into neighboring Dagestan, the mostly Muslim republic, firmly within the Russian Federation, on the Caspian Sea.[27] A caviar-rich republic the size of the Austria, Dagestan is a complex mélange of obscure ethnic groups—more than thirty in all—long ruled by Soviet-bred officials loyal to Moscow. The rebels, several hundred by the best estimates, marched in broad daylight, two by two, well armed with grenade launchers, wearing new camouflage uniforms. When they seized a handful of Dagestani villages across the border, in Moscow the move was seen as an attempt to fulfill an old vow to unite Chechnya with Dagestan in an Islamic state that would reach the Caspian.

The remote stretch of Dagestan had long been a center for the Wahhabi movement. Sergei Stepashin, the Russian prime minister at the time of the incursion, had even once visited the villages under Wahhabi "occupation." In August 1998 Stepashin, then Yeltsin's interior minister, had gone to Dagestan to hear grievances from the village elders. He left convinced that "the Wahhabis are peaceful people, we can work with them." The day after Basayev and Khattab entered Dagestan, Stepashin again flew to Dagestan. This time as prime minister he spoke in stern tones. He said he'd come to take charge, but his face was ash gray. The next day, August 9, 1999, Yeltsin sacked him.

Stepashin had personified loyalty, long considered the president's favorite attribute. However, this was not just another of Yeltsin's seasonal cabinet cleanings. Stepashin's shortcoming, said Oleg Sysuev, a Kremlin aide at the time, was that "he had a heart." Yeltsin needed more than fidelity; he needed strength. He turned to Putin, who had been his FSB director for only a year, and named him prime minister. In eighteen months Yeltsin had sacked five prime ministers. This time, however, he added a shocker. He spoke on television of Putin as his successor. At the time the former KGB officer was unknown. Polls put his popularity ratings at less than 2 percent. The dynamics, however, of the political vacuum had been proved. "Yeltsin could put anyone in the prime minister's job," said Aleksandr Oslon, Russia's best pollster, "and his numbers would rise."

Putin's numbers were aided by more than his new seat of power. The August march into Dagestan, fixed on Russian television screens as a slap in the Kremlin's face, gave him a perfect opportunity to avenge the mistakes of the past. But Putin wanted more: to permit Russia, insulted and injured after the crash of 1998 and burdened by Yeltsin's calcified rule, to imagine itself again a *velikaya derzhava*, a great power. Moscow dispatched helicopter gunships to pound the mud villages the rebels had seized. Basayev and Khattab, however, and nearly all their men, it seemed, had already fled. The new prime minister promised a short operation—he would mercilessly cleanse Dagestan, but under no condition reignite the embers in Chechnya.

During his brief tenure as FSB chief Putin had hung a portrait of Peter the Great in his Lubyanka office. In his first months as prime minister, his aides liked to assure foreign reporters that Peter, the tsar who opened Russia to the West, was Putin's model. Yet Peter had also begun his career with an onslaught against the heathens in the south, conquering the port of Azov in 1696 from the Ottoman Turks, gaining access, after a failed attempt the previous year, to the Black Sea.

For years, in Russian politics the month of August seemed to carry a curse. Both the coup of 1991 and the crash of 1998 came in August. But August 1999 hit Yeltsin particularly hard. His physical and mental health had moved from a topic of concern to ridicule among the Moscow elite. Worse still, scandals brewed on several fronts, conspiring to ruin his fishing vacation. There was the Mabetex mess, a tangled affair that reeked of money laundering on a massive scale and of egregious—even by Russian standards—bribery. The Mabetex story, gaining ground since the spring, had already ensnared Pavel Borodin, the president's drinking partner and chief of one of the state's largest internal empires, the Kremlin Property Department. In August the scandal threatened to drag in Yeltsin's two daughters, their spouses, and a host of family consiglieri. Borodin was alleged to have accepted bribes from a

Kosovar Albanian, Behgjet Pacolli, for multibillion-dollar contracts to refurbish the Kremlin.[28]

August also brought a second scandal, the Bank of New York affair. The story, which first appeared in the *New York Times* on August 19, 1999, alleged that Russian crime bosses, in cahoots with Moscow officials, had washed "as much as ten billion dollars" through the U.S. banking system.[29] The BoNY scandal unfolded as Russian forces bombed and shelled the Wahhabi villages in Dagestan. Then, on August 25, the *Corriere della Sera* ran a detailed exposé of the Mabetex case that linked, for the first time, the Yeltsin family to the misdeeds.

Six days later the bombing season began. Days after the rebels had retreated from Dagestan, a series of bombings rocked Russia. On August 31, as Mia and I sat in an Indian café two blocks away, a bomb exploded in one of Luzhkov's proudest creations, the Manezh, a subterranean shopping mall next to the Kremlin. Placed beside a video arcade, the device wounded forty-one. Two later died from their burns. On September 4, 1999, an apartment building housing Russian officers and their families in the Dagestani town of Buinaksk exploded in the middle of the night. Sixty-two died. Back in Moscow, one after another on September 9 and 13, massive chemical bombs leveled two whole apartment blocks. Three days later a fourth building blew, this time in the south, in the town of Volgodonsk. By then nearly 300 people had been killed in their sleep. Yeltsin denounced the "barbaric acts of terror."

No one came forward to claim responsibility. But the prime suspects naturally were the Chechens. Few facts surfaced, but, as always, theories in Moscow swirled. *Rossiiskaya gazeta*, the daily newspaper of the Russian state, saw a host of possible culprits: Chechen rebels, who "want[ed] to create a great state in the Caucasus," global oil barons, "who want[ed] to redraw the map of a rich region in their favor," and Russophobes, who wanted Moscow to "sink into local conflicts and retire from the world stage." Viktor Ilyukhin, the chairman of the Duma Security Committee and an unreconstructed Communist prone to fulminating without facts, saw the bombings as a Kremlin campaign to bring down Mayor Luzhkov. *Moskovskii komsomolets*, Russia's best-read tabloid and the newspaper closest to Luzhkov, accused his archfoe Berezovsky of masterminding the invasion into Dagestan. The paper even aired an accusation that many—members of the military included—

feared true: that the FSB had set the bombs. No evidence, however, surfaced that the blasts were the work of Chechen extremists.[30]

Questions lingered. There was the choice of targets–working-class districts–and the timing–just when things seemed quiet–and the fact that the Chechens had never set off a bomb in Moscow during the first war. Most disconcerting of all was a strange episode in Ryazan, a city 130 miles southeast of Moscow. On the night of September 22, 1999, just six days after the Volgodonsk bombing, residents of a twelve-story apartment house at 14/16 Novosyelov Street called the police. A bus driver had seen two men carrying something into the basement and feared it was a bomb. The police discovered three sacks bound by wires and a detonator set to go off before dawn. They evacuated the building and called the bomb squad. The next day Putin declared that "vigilance" had thwarted a "terrorist threat." On September 24, 1999, however, in the glare of the television lights, the new head of the FSB, Nikolai Patrushev, a man Putin had brought from Petersburg, apologized. The security service, he said, had put the sacks there itself. It was only "a training exercise," Patrushev said awkwardly. The sacks, he insisted, were filled with sugar.[31]

The bombings, coupled with the invasion of Dagestan, united the nation–against the Chechens. By September's close Putin's War had begun. Russian troops, this time a force of nearly a hundred thousand, were back in Chechnya. This war, the new prime minister vowed, would be different. Moscow would restore order in the lawless region that had enjoyed de facto, if not de jure, independence since driving the Russian forces out after the 1994–96 war. The first campaign had been a humiliation riddled with political indecision and military incompetence. The second round, as one of its architects, General Troshev, promised early, would be "a merciless battle, with Moscow refusing to abstain from any of our weapons, for every square foot of the Chechen republic."

Led by the new strongman in the Kremlin, Russian troops moved with purpose across the northern plains of Chechnya. On television Russians watched with pride, and muted amazement, as Chechen village after Chechen town fell without a shot. When Gudermes fell without a fight, Moscow imagined the war was won. "Only mop-up work remains to be done," announced Putin's unctuous spokesman for the war, Sergei Yastrzhembsky. A spin doctor who had served both Yeltsin and his rival

Luzhkov, Yastrzhembsky held daily briefings to assure reporters the new campaign was an "antiterrorist operation" not a war. "It will be over within days," he promised as New Year's 1999 neared. In the first war Russia's fledgling private media had tested their independence. This time, however, the state drew a new line: To report from the Chechen side was to support the enemy. The local media largely complied, glossing over reports of civilian massacres and Chechen resistance.

In Moscow the politicians and generals now tried to downplay the fate of Grozny. In the first war the city had become known among the troops as a meat grinder. The rebels had mastered the art of urban guerrilla warfare, using underground passages and fortified buildings to entrap Russian tank columns and destroy them. "Grozny is not critical," insisted General Valery Manilov, the logorrheic spokesman for the high command. "We will not storm Grozny" became his mantra at weekly briefings, as reporters wondered how the Russians could win the war without entering the capital.

The answer was simple—and brutal. Early in Putin's War, Aleksandr Zhilin, a former MiG pilot and one of the keenest military journalists in Moscow, mapped the new strategy for me. "You take up positions as far away from your target as possible," Zhilin said, "and shell the hell out of them. You use jets, attack helicopters, artillery—whatever has lead and metal and flies. You hit them day and night without pause. You send in men only once you've leveled everything." The onslaught was calculated to lose as few Russian soldiers as possible, while killing as many Chechens, armed or not, as possible. "Costly in terms of hardware," Zhilin called the plan, "but effective."

Almost immediately the Chechens felt the difference from the first war. This time they fled. At one point more than three hundred thousand abandoned the republic. While most went to Ingushetia, some went south—on foot across the mountains to Georgia. In October 1999 in Duisi, a village at the mouth of the Pankisi Gorge across the border in Georgia, I found hundreds of Chechen refugees crowded in an abandoned hospital.[32] For days they had walked in deep snow, beneath Russian bombers. At times the road was no more than a narrow path, much of it mined. They were the lucky ones, they said. Dozens more had died along the way. During World War II Leningrad residents trapped by the Nazi siege escaped on an ice road across Lake Ladoga to the north of the city. The Soviets later named it the Road of

Life. The road from Grozny into the Pankisi Gorge, the Chechen refugees said, had been a Road of Death.

The refugees had no trouble recognizing the Kremlin's new tactics. "In the first war," said Roza, a nine-year-old girl from Urus-Martan, "we'd sit in the cellar and count the bombs." But in the new war, she said, "there are so many you can't even count them." The hospital, long abandoned, had no heat. Plastic sheets hung over the empty window-frames. Khassan, a village elder from Samashki, spoke of a new level of brutality. "I never imagined I'd feel nostalgia for Yeltsin," he said. "I never imagined war could be worse than what we saw before. But this is not war. It is murder on a state level; it is mass murder."

Despite the generals' assurances, few in Moscow doubted that the Russians would have to storm Grozny. This time, however, Kremlin officials were sure the city would fall easily. After all, little of its infrastructure remained, and given the mass flight of refugees, this time around there would be few civilians to shelter the rebels. By November 1999 Russian forces had invested the city, hoping to sever the supply lines to the last Chechen fighters within it. The siege had begun.

By December 1999 the so-called *chastniye sektora* (private districts), the stretches of little single-story houses that had spread around Grozny in the years since Gorbachev, had been scorched. The tall apartment buildings along the long avenues were now shells, dark eye sockets in the city's skull. The center, leveled once in the first war, had fallen silent. Civilians, both Chechen and Russian, still lived in Grozny. No one knew how many remained—some said as many as twenty thousand—but they were invisible. Day and night they crowded together in dank cellars beneath the ruins.

The siege lasted 102 days. On January 31, after two weeks of the second war's bloodiest fighting, Minutka Square, the intersection long considered the key to the city, fell. There was in the end no great battle for Grozny. Both sides exaggerated the numbers they had killed and wounded. However, the Chechen fighters, even the generals in Moscow had to admit, made a strong stand. Some had retreated earlier to their traditional refuge, the mountains south of Grozny. In the final days of January 2000, the last rebel contingent in the city, some three thousand men in all, started to decamp. They moved at night, in two columns through a corridor on the city's southwestern side.

By February 1 the fighters, now several hundred fewer in number, had reached the village of Alkhan-Kala, eleven miles southwest of Aldy. Fighters who survived the trek later told me how they crossed frozen pastures covered with mines. Knowing the fields were mined, they moved forward one after another, in a suicide walk. "We shall see each other in paradise," they screamed as they stepped out into the field. *"Allah akbar!"* others cried. As they walked, explosions, feet triggering mines, lit the darkness. "The only way to cross the field," said a young Chechen who was there that night, "was to walk across the bodies." The exodus cost the fighters several top commanders. Basayev lost his right foot to a mine. Among the dead was Lecha Dudayev, the mayor of Grozny and nephew of the late former leader Dudayev.

Every village the retreating fighters passed through became the object of fierce Russian bombing: Shaami-Yurt, Katyr-Yurt, Gekhi-Chu. Aldy had suffered surprisingly little damage—before February. Bombs and shells had fallen on the village, hitting scattered houses and the train station. But it had not figured in any clashes between the Russian forces and the rebels. Only later did I piece it together. On their bloody retreat from the besieged capital to Alkhan-Kala, one column of fighters had come straight through Aldy.

GRIM AS IT WAS, Gudermes became home. In Moscow the town was considered under Russian control. In reality, the Russians' hold here was as illusive as in any other corner of Chechnya. The officers kept to their barracks, a Soviet-style housing project laced with several cordons of fortifications. Even still, their sleep was routinely interrupted by grenades, remote-controlled bombs, and Kalashnikov fire. In the local bazaar stocked by Dagestani merchants, Russian soldiers shopped warily, moving only in packs. Moscow's Chechen proxies, however, the natives recruited in the latest pacification effort, may have had the most to fear. Akhmed Kadirov, once the grand mufti of the republic, now Putin's choice to rule it, lived in Gudermes, but no one ever saw him. They only heard him—each morning and evening, coming and going in a Russian helicopter. "The invisible mufti," the Chechens called him mockingly.

Issa's apartment had all the warmth of an IRA safe house. He liked to keep the windows papered over, visitors at a minimum, and his Makarov pistol handy. The apartment was a gift from Nikolai Koshman, a feckless

Russian apparatchik who had risen in the Railways Ministry and had served as a deputy in the brief puppet regime Moscow had tried to foist on Chechnya during the first war.[33] In the new campaign, before settling on the former mufti Kadirov, Putin had recalled Koshman to duty, naming him his viceroy in the republic.

By his own estimation, Issa was equal parts Chechen and Soviet. Every morning he slapped on French cologne and prayed to Allah. Each night he prayed again. Yet when time and resources permitted, he drank. His usual drink, as beer and wine ran scarce in Chechnya, was *spirt*, denatured ethyl alcohol. As a reward for his taking on Dudayev, Moscow in 1995 had given him a sinecure, a position atop the Foreign Relations Department in Russia's puppet regime of Doku Zavgayev, a Soviet bureaucrat and Chechen loyalist. At one point Issa headed the negotiations for seven hundred million dollars' worth of contracts for the reconstruction of Grozny. Mabetex, the Swiss-based construction firm that had brought the Yeltsin family a flood of bad press, had a five-million-dollar slice of them. Issa was proud of his snapshots, pictures of himself in Grozny with Pacolli, the Kosovar Albanian who ran Mabetex. The Turkish firm Enka had been the lead partner. But it had all been run through Borodin. Nothing of course had come of it. "Only more war," Issa said. "And more reason to hate the Russians and distrust your fellow Chechens."

Early in Putin's War, Moscow had again turned to Issa. The Russians made him an aide to Koshman, with the promise of his old job back at Grozneft. By then he had made the rebels' blacklist, an honor bestowed on him by Movladi Udugov, Dudayev's onetime minister of ideology who had long since gone underground and now ran Basayev's and Khattab's multilingual Web site, Kavkaz.org. The rebels, Issa explained, had sentenced their enemies to death under *Shari'a*. With pride he proffered the list of names. Yeltsin topped it, but there, just a few lines below Putin, was Issa. He had few socially acceptable things to say about Udugov, Basayev, and Khattab. However, after six months of Putin's War, and hopeless attempts to work with his generals— Vladimir Shamanov, Ivan Babichev, Viktor Kazantsev, and Gennadi Troshev— he had even fewer nice things to say about the Russians.

Early one morning before the heat of the sun started to fill the apartment, we rose and, without tea, climbed into the UAZik. We drove slowly through Gudermes on its rutted roads. Scattering stray dogs, we creaked past the half-guarded officers' headquarters, beside the string of forlorn stalls that now pretended to be the local bazaar, and through the first checkpoints of the morning. We left town and headed west, following the old asphalt through brown fields, until at the eastern edge of Grozny, we came to Khankala, the Russian military headquarters in Chechnya. Journalists who had covered the war in Vietnam said Khankala reminded them of Da Nang. The base seemed like a small town. Everywhere tents and helicopters stretched as far as you could see.

We continued on, coming again to the ruins of Minutka Square, then on into the center of Grozny. The streets were as empty as before. In the concrete remains nothing stirred. Not cats, not dogs. Every so often, among the burned shells of the apartment houses, flecks of color flashed. Clothes dried on a line strung between two walls that a shell had opened to the street. The city's water supply was tainted with disease. There was no plumbing and no electricity, no shops and no transport, but someone did, after all, live here. Chechens, men, women, and their children, were coming home.

At a barren corner, near where the old Presidential Palace once stood, young girls sold candy, gum, and glass jars filled with home-distilled kerosene. They stood by their wares but didn't smile or wave. They had no customers. The only people moving among them were soldiers. They did not walk. They traveled on top of their tanks, trucks, and APCs. Only at the checkpoints did the soldiers, bare-chested in the hot sun, stand.

Issa hated taking lip from young Russians with Kalashnikovs. But they were becoming harder to avoid. "You take the same route twice in one day," he said. "If there's no checkpoint the first time, it's there the next time you go by." Amid the ruins the checkpoints often marked what had once been city blocks. The Russians stopped each car, scoured the occupants' papers and searched the trunk. They feared the suicide bombers who had taken to blowing up their checkpoints and barracks with regularity. The tactic of turning your body into a bomb may have come from the Middle East, but the Chechens made a significant advancement in the technique. Long before Palestinian women and girls joined the bombers' ranks, Chechen women had done so. Issa was never happy at the checkpoints. But the worst, he would later say, had been the last one we'd negotiated that morning, the final checkpoint before Aldy.

NINE

OFFICIALLY IT IS A district of Grozny, but to its residents Aldy is a village. Once it had its own bakery, clinic, library, and bazaar, where the locals sold vegetables. In those days, at School No. 39, nearly a thousand children studied each day. That was all before the first war in Chechnya, back when nearly ten thousand people lived in Aldy. The village lies in the Zavodskoi (factory) district of Grozny. Whoever worked back then, hardly the majority, worked at the plants across the way, producing petroleum and chemicals, cement and bricks. Now, under banners of black clouds, the factories nearly blended into the surrounding ruins. Some stood out. They were still burning.

Aldy sits above a dam, across from Grozny's largest reservoir. The village comprises a broad rectangle of a dozen streets lined with squat single-story houses, each with its own sheltered courtyard. In the middle of thick greenery, the branches of old trees—apricot, pear, cherry, peach, apple, walnut—twist above the low roofs. Bound together by fences of metal and wood taller than a man, the yards appear linked in a line against the world outside.

Inside, on the other side of the fences, the survivors of the massacre were still numb. Bislan Ismailov, a soft-spoken Chechen in his forty-second year, spoke in a detached monotone. His eyes were fixed on me, but his mind was not here. He was there. For him, February 5, 2000, was not fixed in time. When he spoke of it, he switched tenses without cause. Bislan had not left Aldy. He had been here throughout. Once he'd worked at the fuel plant across the way. Back in the days of Brezhnevian slumber he'd become an engineer. But throughout Russia's second war in Chechnya, he had collected, washed, and helped bury the dead.

"For months that's all I did," he said. "Whoever they bring in, we bury them. Eight, ten, twelve people a day. They brought in fighters and left them. Have to bury them? Have to. They bring them in beat-up, shot-up cars from the center of town . . . and we buried them, right here by our house, in the yard of the clinic. Right here, sixty-three people—all before February."

Bislan was thin but not frail. He had dark almond-shaped eyes and long black lashes. His thin black mustache was neatly trimmed. His appearance was impeccable. In fact he struck me, given the words that poured from his mouth, as inordinately clean.

In the last days of January 2000, a few weeks after the New Year's Day when the Western world breathed with relief at having survived the millennial turn without catastrophe and Putin, in his first hours as acting president, flew to Chechnya to award hunting knives to the troops and tell them their task was to keep the Russian Federation intact, the Chechen fighters had abandoned Grozny. In Aldy, life by then had taken on a strange, brutal routine as it had in nearly every other corner of the city. The nights were filled with shelling, and the mornings brought only more of the encroaching thunder.

"They fired everything they could," Bislan said. "Bombs, missiles, grenades. They shot from all sides. There were times when we could not collect the dead. We would bury them days later."

On the morning of February 3 nearly a hundred of the men in Aldy decided to take action. They left their homes and cellars and walked to the neighboring district of Grozny, District 20. They carried torn bits of white sheets as flags and went in search of the commander of the Russian troops, the ones closest to Aldy. They wanted to plead with him to stop the shelling, to assure him they were sheltering no fighters. As the group crossed the field of frozen mud where the Russians had dug their positions, shots were fired. One of the villagers fell to the ground. His name was Nikolai. He happened to be an ethnic Russian.

Until then the villagers had not seen a single Russian soldier during the second war, but in the middle of the afternoon on February 4 the first troops arrived. They were not friendly, but they were "businesslike." The first group of soldiers came to warn them. They were *srochniki*, conscripts, drafted into the war. They were young, the villagers recalled, almost polite. "So young the beards were barely on their cheeks," said Bislan. They wore dirty uniforms, and their faces were covered with mud. They were exhausted. They went house to house, telling the men and women of Aldy to get prepared. "Get out of your cellars," they said. "Don't hide and don't go out in the street. Get your passports ready," they said. For the next soldiers to check. "Because we're not the bad guys," they said. "The bad guys come after us."

On the next morning, the morning of February 5, the villagers, some seven hundred who remained, sleeping in old coats and blankets in cramped basements, heard something strange. As first light came, and the slopes of the snowy peaks far to the south brightened, as they rolled their prayer rugs out toward Mecca, bent to their knees, and praised Allah, they heard silence. No thunderclaps. Only the sounds of chickens, sheep, and cows. The numbing monotony had broken. The shelling had stopped.

For months the families of Aldy had waited. For months they had been transfixed by one question. They knew the Russians had surrounded Grozny; they only wondered when the attack would come. For days they had stored water from a nearby spring and kept the few fish the men could catch, the *belyi nalym* that once grew three feet long in the reservoir, frozen under the snow. When the Russians come, they thought, it would be good not to go out. The silence disturbed them, but they welcomed an hour for urgent repairs.

Bislan climbed up onto the low roof of his single-story house with a hammer and three scraps of plastic sheeting. From the roof he saw that his neighbor Salaudi, a mechanic in his forties, had done the same. Salaudi, deaf since birth, had done better. He'd found a sheet of aluminum siding. He was trying to nail it over a hole the shelling had left.

At just after nine, smoky layers of chill mist still blanketed the corners of Grozny. Aldy sits up high. It commands a vantage point over the lowlands that edge the city. But Bislan could not yet see the sun. He only heard the shouts. From the northern end of the village, APCs churned the asphalt of Matasha-Mazayeva. Three bus stops long, Matasha-Mazayeva is Aldy's central street, the only one that runs the length of the village. At the same time, the Russians came along the frozen mud of the parallel streets, Almaznaya and Tsimlyanskaya. Still more men and armored vehicles filled the roads that run perpendicular, Khoperskaya, Uralskaya, and Kamskaya. Within minutes the village was clogged with APCs and, running on each side of them, more than one hundred soldiers.

They did not all wear the same uniforms. Some wore camouflage. Some wore white snow ponchos. Some wore only undershirts or were naked to their waists. Nearly all wore dark camouflage trousers covered in dirt. Some had scarves wrapped around their necks, and some bandannas. Some wore knit hats pulled down close to their eyes. Some had tattoos on their arms, necks, and hands. Some carried five-liter canisters, marked only with numbers stenciled onto the plastic. But they all carried Kalashnikovs.

These were not *srochniki*, the conscripts of the day before. These were *kontraktniki*, contract soldiers. The distance between the two is vast. Conscripts stand on the far edge of puberty, often just a few months over eighteen. Contract soldiers, however, are older, more experienced, and fighting for the money. They earn much more than the newly drafted soldiers, and they are in the main far more battle hardened.

Kontraktniki were easy to spot, Shvedov said. "They look like criminals." With their shaved heads, bandannas, tattoos, and muscles, they tended to look like convicts who had spent too much time on the prison yard weights.

At the edges of Aldy, the soldiers had parked APCs and olive drab trucks whose open flatbeds sat high off the ground. They had blocked all the exits, sealed off the village.

Bislan was nailing the plastic sheet onto his roof when he heard the first screams. He looked down Matasha-Mazayeva, to the houses at the northernmost corner of the village. Two plumes of blue-gray smoke swirled there. The screams grew louder. He clung to his roof and looked down the other end of Aldy. Smoke had begun to billow as well at the southern end of the village. House by house, from either end, the men were moving down Matasha-Mazayeva. House by house they tried to get into the locked courtyards. First they kicked the gates with their boots. When that failed, they shot the locks.

The killing began at the northern edge of the village, on Irtyshskaya Street. The Idigovs were among the first to face the Russians. They were brothers, Lom-Ali and Musa. They stood at the door of their uncle's small house and tried to reason with the soldiers. There were a lot of soldiers. Too many. There would be no pleading. They were not listening. They screamed at Lom-Ali and Musa.

"Get in the basement!" one barked.

"Come on!" another yelled. "Don't you want to be in the action film?"

There was no cellar in the house, so the soldiers took them to the house next door. They forced the brothers into the cellar and threw a grenade in. It hit the cold floor and bounced. Lom-Ali, the younger of the brothers, threw himself on the grenade. He was in his late thirties. The shrapnel tore him to bits. Those who collected his body later were certain there must have been more than one grenade. His body had been cut into too many parts. The force of the explosion threw his elder brother, Musa, against the concrete wall. He was knocked unconscious, but came to as the smoke seeped into the basement. He looked for his brother and started to climb out of the cellar.

It was still not yet ten when the men reached the heart of Aldy and started to shoot—in every direction. Smoke and screams filled the air. Bislan climbed down from his roof. He saw people gathering at the corner of Kamskaya and the Fourth Almazny Lane. They had come into the middle of the street to show the soldiers their documents. The soldiers encircled them. They were shooting into the sky, and they were yelling.

"Get out of your houses!" one screamed.

"Go collect your bodies!" another yelled.

Not everyone that morning in Aldy was making repairs. In his small square house on the corner of Matasha-Mazayeva, No. 152, Avalu Sugaipov was making tea. Avalu, like his brothers, was a bus driver. He was forty, and driving a bus was all he had ever done. There was no food for breakfast. He could only put the kettle on. He would make the morning tea for his guests, two strangers who had come from the center of Grozny. One man was in his sixties, the other his late fifties. In Aldy, they had heard, there were still people. Safety, they imagined, was in numbers. Avalu had taken them in. They sat at his small kitchen table, waiting for the water to boil.

A woman, Kaipa, sat with them. No one knew her last name. She and her nine-year-old-daughter, Leila, had come from the town of Djalka. Her husband had died long ago. She had seven other children. The war had scattered them all save her youngest. The shelling in Djalka had become unbearable. They'd moved to another village, and then another, before coming to her mother's house in District 20 next door to Aldy. At the end of December 1999 she came to Aldy. Shamkhan, the mullah, was her distant cousin.

Avalu lived in his mother's house. His mother and younger brother had gone to Nazran in November. There were two small houses here—six rooms and a cellar in all. Avalu took in Kaipa and her girl, Leila. They had been living in the second house for a week now.

As Avalu poured the tea, they heard the screams. The men did not want her to, but Kaipa went out. They rushed after her. Just as she stepped out into the courtyard, the soldiers lowered their guns. Kaipa was hit twice, in the head and chest.

"Mama jumped in the air and then fell to the ground," nine-year-old Leila would later say.

The next bullets hit the two men. They were shot in the face.

Avalu stood at the threshold of his house and held the little girl tight. He told her to go back into the house, and he took a step forward. She turned around and saw his body leap into the air, too. Avalu fell backward, into the house.

Leila ran through the house to the room in its farthest corner. She crawled under the bed and hid behind a sack of onions. She lay there in silence as two soldiers entered the house.

"Pour it," one said.

She heard something splash against the floor.

"But where's the girl?" the other asked.

"Don't kill me," Leila said, coming out from under the bed.

One of them lifted her out. He covered her eyes with a scarf and, stepping around the bodies, carried her from the house. In the yard, from under the cloth, she saw her mother, lying facedown in a circle of blood. In the street he put a can of meat in her hands. He tried to calm her down. He looked up and found two women staring at him.

"Take her," he told them, and returned to the courtyard of the house.

The house was already on fire. The women grabbed the girl and ran to the far side of Matasha-Mazayeva. Every night for weeks the girl would need a shot of sedatives to sleep.

BISLAN WAITED FOR the soldiers to turn the corner before he opened the metal gate of his house. He crossed the street and walked into Avalu's yard. That was when he saw the bodies: two men, badly burned, one shot in the eye, and a woman. Bislan had known Kaipa. He stepped into the house. There, he saw the body of his friend Avalu, lying faceup in the middle of his kitchen. Bislan looked around the kitchen. The teapot sat on the stove, the cups on the table.

ASET CHADAYEVA RAN from her family's house on the Fourth Almazny Lane. She threw open the gate and ran into the street. She had heard the APCs, but when the screams grew close, she could wait no longer. There in the street, some thirty feet to the right, four houses down, she saw two Russian officers. They were staring up at Salaudi, the deaf mechanic who persisted in trying to fix his roof.

"Look at that idiot," one said.

"Bring him down," yelled the other.

As one of the soldiers raised his rifle, Aset screamed, "He can't hear you! He's deaf!"

The soldier turned toward her and fired.

"Get on the ground!" they yelled.

Aset fell to her knees. The days had warmed since January. In the first days of February the snow had even begun to melt. The ground was icy and black, half-frozen mud. Her younger brother Akhyad, who'd turned twenty-five weeks earlier, ran from the house. "Come here and show us your documents!" the soldiers screamed. Aset and Akhyad walked slowly, arms in the air, toward the men. As they went through Akhyad's papers, Aset measured the men's faces. One, she sensed, was the commander. Aset's father and brother Timur came out into the street. They pleaded with the commander to let Aset and Akhyad go. Several more soldiers joined the two in the middle of the street. One of them screamed curses at Aset, her brothers, and her father. Tall and reeking of vodka, he stuck the barrel of his Kalashnikov into her ribs, pushed her to the fence.

The commander had had enough. *"Svolochi!"* he yelled at his own men. "You bastards! Get the fuck out of here! Move it!"

Aset saw an opportunity. There were still many people in the houses, she said. "I can collect them," she told the commander. "I can bring them to you. That way," she said, "your men can check their documents faster." Timur, Akhyad, and their father said they'd stay with the soldiers if the commander let Aset gather their neighbors.

He agreed but turned to Timur. "Walk behind me," he ordered.

"Don't worry," Timur said. "Our people won't shoot you."

The commander looked at Timur. "But mine might," he said.

Aset went down all the houses on Fourth Almazny Lane and on the side streets left and right. She came back with a crowd, two dozen women, men, and children. The soldiers pushed them forward, out into the intersection of Kamskaya and Fourth Almazny.

"You'll stand here," they said, "until we're through."

The commander came close to Aset. She was carrying as always a green plastic bag. In its folds, a gray wolf, the symbol of the Chechen people, howled. It was the flag of Ichkeria, the free state Dudayev had founded.

"What's in the bag?" he asked.

Aset had spent the war in Aldy. She too had helped bury the dead. She had collected the bodies, and body parts, and washed them for burial by the mullah Shamkhan. She was a nurse. She had finished her nursing studies at Grozny's medical college in 1987, in the heyday of Gorbachev and glasnost. She had worked in a children's clinic in Grozny until December 1994, until the Russians first stormed Grozny. In Putin's War, at thirty-two, she had become a one-woman paramedic unit. Day and night for months she had nursed the wounded and foraged to feed Aldy's elderly and sick. She had prepared food for her neighbors, both Chechen and the few stranded Russians, old men and women who had nowhere to go. She had also tended the fighters. They brought medicine from their fortified basements in the city and fish from the nearby reservoir. When the fighters passed through, she had sewn them up. She had cleaned their wounds—with *spirt*—pulled the metal from their flesh, and sent them on their way. Aset had feared the day they would abandon the city, and when at last they did, it was the first time in Putin's War that she cried.

"Bandages, medicine, syringes," Aset answered the commander. "I am a nurse."

"Then you can help me," he said.

He grabbed her by the sleeve and pulled her close, away from the crowd gathered at the corner.

"There's been a mistake," he said. "Some of my men have killed some of your men. They've got to be covered up quickly."

She looked at him but did not understand.

The commander had blue eyes and light hair. He was neither tall nor short. He was average, Aset said. "A typical, average Russian man." As she stood next to the commander, his radio crackled. Across the static, she heard a soldier's call name—*Kaban*—clearly: "Come in Boar, come in." In the street his men had shouted the names Dima and Sergei.

The commander seemed stunned. "What the hell are you assholes doing?" he screamed into his radio. "Have you lost your minds?" He looked at Aset and said, almost softly, "Stay with me. Don't leave my side. Or they'll kill you too."

At the corner the men and women and children stood still. They stood close to one another. They did not move from the corner. They stood there, as the smoke grew thick, for nearly two hours.

IN MOSCOW THAT SAME Saturday afternoon I had heard on Ekho Moskvy, the liberal news radio station of the Gusinsky media empire, that in the settlement of Aldy on the southern edge of Grozny a *zachistka* was under way. To many Russians, the word, meaning "a little cleanup," resonated with positive overtones. It meant "they're cleaning out the bandits." By the time Aldy burned and bled, *zachistka* operations had become routine, a staple in the "counterterrorist operation." A *zachistka*, it was understood, was a house-to-house search for members of the armed opposition. Broadcast on television back home, the endeavor was meant to impress. On the evening news the footage resembled scenes from American real crime shows. Russian soldiers moved house to house in search of bandits, not unlike the cops, guns drawn, who sidle down crack house corridors to ferret out dealers. On the ground the news carried a different meaning.

BISLAN KEPT RUNNING. He went to the next house on Matasha-Mazayeva, No. 160. The Magomadov brothers, Salman and Abdullah, lived here. Flames licked at the porch and the roof above it. He looked left and right. Three houses in a row were on fire. Salman was sixty, Abdullah fifty-three. Bislan had seen them the day before.

The stench of burning filled the winter air. Bislan could not find the Magomadovs in the yard. The Russians set the basements on fire first. He knew that, but he could not get through the front door. It was already aflame. He knew the brothers were in there. The stench was so strong. Then he heard the screams. Bislan broke a side window and climbed in, but in the dense smoke he became disoriented. He could see nothing. A staircase led to the basement, but he couldn't find it. He couldn't even find the window again. He ran to a wall, felt the glass pane and smashed it. He pulled himself through and fell into the yard.

The remains of the Magomadov brothers were found days later. They had been in the cellar. Both had been shot and then set afire. In the yard, to the right of the front door, bullet casings were on the ground. Among the ashes in the basement were bullets from 5.45-mm and 7.62-mm automatic rifles, the new and old standard-issue Kalashnikovs. There was also a wristwatch. It had stopped at eleven twenty-five.

Next door, in front of No. 162, Gula Khaidaev was already dead. He had left his house and been shot before he could step onto the street. Maybe he had heard the screams; maybe he had come out to show his passport. He was seventy-six. Shot three times, in his knee, chest, and forehead, Gula still held his passport in his outstretched hand. A few feet away lay his cousin Rakat Akhmadova. She had been shot in the neck and chest. She was eighty-two.

Malika Khumidovna, a widowed schoolteacher in her forties, who had guided a generation of Aldy children through School No. 39, stood with her back to a wall in the yard of a house on Khopyorskaya Street. Her three girls and mother stood near her. So did thirteen other women. They had slept and eaten together in the basement of the house. It was large, and they had kept glass jars filled with water and *kompot*, homemade fruit juice, there. Up until the day before, there had been many more women and children here. In January as many as thirty had slept in the cellar.

The soldiers had told them to stand at the cement wall, in the cold. Hours passed. The women dared not move. They stood there, their backs to the wall. The soldiers brought chairs out of the house and sat across from the women. Two soldiers ventured in the cellar and found the jars of *kompot* the women had kept there. They emerged with smiles and passed the sweet drink among themselves. Every so often the soldiers shot into the wall. The bullet holes traced an arc a few feet above the heads of the women and their daughters.

When their squad leader came upon the scene, he yelled. He told the men to get rid of the women. The soldiers went to work. Two took the children aside, while one led the women into an abandoned house next door.

Malika had already said her prayers. She had asked Allah not for mercy but to light her path. She did not look at the soldier. She averted her eyes. As the women walked into the house, the soldier stuffed a note into her hand. On the paper, he said, was his home address. He told Malika not to worry. He wasn't going to shoot her or any of the women. She reminded him, he said, of his mother. "So write my mama," he said. "Tell her I didn't kill you."

BISLAN PASSED TWO houses before he entered the yard of No. 170, nearly tripping on the first body. Just by the gate, half on the road, half in the yard, lay Rizvan Umkhaev, a seventy-two-year-old pensioner who in recent years had guarded the parking lot of the TB hospital in Grozny. The bullets had ripped right through him. Issa Akhmadov, a short, muscular man who at thirty-five had never held a job and spent too many years in jail, lay near him. It had been a close-range execution. They, too, still clutched their passports.

Bislan turned toward the house and took two steps forward. He could go no farther. Behind him lay the ghastly remains of Sultan Temirov, whose head had been blown off. He was forty-nine. His body was mangled, destroyed by a mass of metal. His head would never be found.

A few steps on, behind the high metal fence of No. 140, seventy-two-year-old Magomed Gaitaev lay dead. He had driven a tractor in the fields beyond the reservoir his whole life. He had lived for years alone. A bullet had pierced the base of his neck and torn his left cheek open as it exited. His chest pocket was open. It held his passport. His glasses hung on the top of the gate to his house.

Across the road, a scene had unfolded that revealed that the villagers were not the only ones afraid. Malika Labazanova, a plump round-faced woman in her forties who wore her dark brown hair in a bun, stood between two soldiers and her front door. They told her they wanted only to search her house. She opened the door. Once they checked the house, one of the soldiers turned to Malika and raised his gun at her. She fell to her knees and pleaded.

He stood over her in the front room of her house and said, "Lie down and don't move."

He shot into the air. If anyone knew, he said, that he had not killed her, he'd be killed as well.

At No. 1 Podolskaya Street, a ten-minute walk from the center of Aldy, the terror struck mercilessly. Sixty-seven-year-old Khasmagomed Estamirov, a disabled former chauffeur, had sent his wife, two daughters, and toddler grandson away to the refugee camps of Ingushetia. But the rest of his clan was home: his cousin Said-Akhmed Masarov; his son, Khozh-Akhmad, who had returned to care for his ailing father; and his daughter-in-law, Toita. At twenty-nine, Toita was eight and one-half months into her third pregnancy. Her one-year-old, Khassan, was also with them. He had taken his first steps that week.

By noon his older brother, Khusein, the toddler who had been sent off to the camps of Ingushetia, had been orphaned. The soldiers had killed everyone in the Estamirov house. The old man. The little boy. His pregnant mother. They even killed the family cow. It was trapped when the soldiers set everything they saw aflame. They torched the yard and the house. They burned the family car as well. Then, as the flames engulfed the cow alive, they left.

Khasmagomed's cousin found the bodies. As he approached the burning house, a mud-splattered APC was driving away. Father and son lay in the yard, side by side. Khasmagomed had been shot in the chest, several times. His wallet was on the ground, empty. The corpses were burned. Toita and her little boy Khassan lay under the awning in the courtyard on the concrete floor. The concrete was pockmarked with bullet holes. Toita, due to give birth in two weeks, was shot in the chest and stomach. Her ring and earrings were gone. Across the threshold to the small house lay the body of the cousin, smoldering. Blood covered the floors and walls.

In the house Khasmagomed had built a small iron stove to keep the family warm. Thirty-two bullet holes had pierced it. Khasmagomed had asked his cousin Said-Akhmed to come live with him. "It's frightening on your own," he had said. "Here we'll be together."

Here, too, the young conscripts had come the day before, February 4. They had warned the Estamirovs. "The *kontraktniki* are coming next," they said. "You'd better leave."

Khasmagomed, a proud grandfather who could count at least seven generations that tied him to the Chechen land, had stayed in the house he had built. He was retired, and his health was bad. But he had earned Hero of Labor medals for his decades of driving Party officials around Grozny. He did not believe the soldiers. He did not think the Russians would do anything. "They'll just come," he told his family, "and check our passports."

He and his wife had remained throughout the first war on Podolskaya Street. They had lost their first house but rebuilt it from the ground. He did not worry about the Russians coming. He believed they would bring order. So as soon as the conscripts left, Khasmogamed and his son went into their yard. They hung white sheets in front of the house, and on the fence, in white paint, they wrote, "*Zachistka* done."

IT WAS NEARING THREE in the afternoon and the sun had still not appeared when the soldiers came back to the center of Aldy, to the Abulkhanov house at No. 145 Matasha-Mazayeva. Five members of the family were living there: the elderly owner, his wife, their daughter-in-law, Luisa, their niece, and her twelve-year-old son, Islam—an old man, three women, and a boy. The soldiers first came early in the morning. They shot the family dog. All day long other soldiers had come—some wore white snowsuits; some had faces so dirty you could see only their eyes.

This time the owner of the house, seventy-one-year-old Akhmed Abulkhanov, tried to give them his passport, but they threw it on the ground. They lined them all up—Abulkhanov, his wife, their niece, her son, Islam, and their daughter-in-law, Luisa—against a wall at the side of the house.

The soldiers swore at them all and grabbed Islam.

"You'll make a good little fighter," one said as he laughed.

"Look, you guys," the old man said, "what are you doing?"

A soldier butted him with his Kalashnikov. They asked for whatever the family had: jewelry, money, wine. The women undid their earrings and surrendered them. The old man said he had no wine in the house and no money. He said if they let him, he'd go borrow money from a neighbor.

Several soldiers went with Abulkhanov as he went to his friend's house, around the corner on Third Tsimlyansky Lane. Khusein Abdulmezhidov, forty-seven, and his elder sister, Zina, both were home. Zina, a short black-haired woman, had turned sixty not long before. For years she had manned the counter at the bakery in Chernorechiye, the adjoining district just across the dam from Aldy.[34] They gave the soldiers all they had, three hundred rubles. It was not enough. There in the yard of his friend's house the soldiers shot Abulkhanov. They did not spare Zina or Khusein. Alongside their neighbor they both were killed in their own yard.

Aldy lay in flames. Black smoke filled the sky, and the stench was heavy. Whatever the liquid was that the soldiers poured on the houses, it burned well. And long. All along Matasha-Mazayeva Street, Aldy's central road, the houses were aflame. Even those villagers whose houses went untouched could only stand and stare as the fires gained force. All the while the screams, wave after wave, continued to rise behind the fences. But they were screams of discovery now—of horror, not pain.

By late afternoon, when the soldiers finally left, the list of the dead was long: at least fifty-two men and eight women. In English we call such an event a massacre. The Russian military command, and the investigators who later exhumed the bodies, persisted in calling it a *zachistka*. Given its privileged place in Putin's War, the term had moved from the front line into the political vernacular. Although the Russian military command likes to translate *zachistka* as a "mop-up operation," the word derives from the verb *chistit'*, meaning "to clean" or "to cleanse." Linguistically, at least, Putin's *zachistki* were related to Stalin's purges, the *chistki*. For Chechens, however, a *zachistka* had little to do with mopping up and everything to do with cleaning out. To them it meant state-sponsored terror, pillage, rape, and murder.

IN MOSCOW THE following day, a quiet snowbound Sunday, sheets of thick flakes, buoyant and motelike, fell steadily and kept the avenues empty and white. No one had yet heard of the horrors wreaked on Aldy, when Putin, now acting president of Russia, went on television to announce the end of the military operation in Grozny.

"As far as the Chechen situation is concerned," he said, "I can tell you that the General Staff has just reported that the last stronghold where terrorists were offering resistance—Grozny's Zavodskoi district—was seized awhile ago and that the Russian flag was raised on one of its administrative buildings."

Grozny's Zavodskoi district is where Aldy lies.

"And so," Putin concluded, "we can say that the operation to liberate Grozny is over."

The troubles, however, were far from over. All that spring and into the summer, when I arrived in Chechnya, the pace of the war may have slowed, but to those on the ground, both Chechen and Russian, it remained as devastating as ever. After the fall of Grozny the Chechen fight-ers turned increasingly to a new tactic, low-intensity, but persistent, guer-rilla warfare. As in the first war, they bought grenades, land mines, and munitions from Russian soldiers–some corrupt, but some just hungry or awake to the grim reality that Putin's War would drag on with or without their patriotic duty. Almost daily Chechen fighters ambushed Russian con-voys, checkpoints, and administrative headquarters. They killed at night and in the day, choosing their targets at random–a clutch of Russian sol-diers buying bread in a local market–or with precision: high-ranking Chechen officials whom Moscow had appointed their administrative prox-ies in the region.

At the same time, the civilian population grew rapidly. By the summer of 2000 more than one hundred thousand Chechens had returned from Ingushetia. They came home to more than destroyed homes and fresh graves. Chechnya was now under Moscow's arbitrary rule. The sweeps continued, and with them, the cases of extrajudicial reprisal. Human rights advocates collected new reports of extortions and beatings, rapes and summary executions. For young male Chechens, however, the primary fear was detention. Each month more and more young men disappeared from the streets. At best the detentions were a rough form of intelligence gathering. At worst they served the enforcers' sadistic urges. But perhaps most commonly, the men were taken hostage merely for ransom. It was also not uncommon that days or weeks later their bodies would be found, dumped at a conveniently empty corner of town.

WE SAT UNDER A TRELLIS heavy with grapevines, in the still, hot air of the narrow courtyard of Aset Chadayeva's home. Aset, the nurse who sur-vived the massacre, was not here, but I handed a note from her to her mother, Hamsat. Aset told me that without it, her parents would not talk. No one would. Such was the fear, she had warned, in Aldy.

"This man is a journalist," Aset had written. "You can trust him. Tell him about the Fifth."

Hamsat had dropped the note and was crying. She wore a dark blouse, a long black skirt faded gray, and a cloth apron around her waist. She wiped her eyes with the end of the apron. Aset's seventy-two-year-old father, Tuma—I recognized him by his great bald head—came into the yard to embrace me. Around us, sisters emerged (Aset was the eldest of seven children), then cousins and grandchildren. In all, there must have been a dozen members of the Chadayev family here, but only Aset's father and brother, Timur, sat at the table with me. Timur was in his early thirties. He wore no shirt, only a well-worn jeans jacket. His ribs were protruding. Beneath his long lashes, his eyeballs bulged slightly. Timur, I knew from Aset, remained in shock. "When you gather the burned pieces of flesh of your friends and neighbors," she had said of her brother, "it affects how you think."

Aset's mother, shifting her weight nervously from her left to her right foot, stood behind her son and husband. Her grandchildren brought bowls of candies wrapped in brightly colored wax paper. Her daughters produced flat, hard pillows for me to sit on.

Tuma wandered the square concrete yard, under the green of the arbor, mumbling to no one in particular. Occasionally he turned in my direction, and I could make out what he was saying. The afternoon, like every afternoon for weeks, was stifling. It must have been over ninety degrees.

"We've never had such heat," Tuma said softly. "Never. Such heat. Look at the grapes."

It was all he could say. He, too, I could see, was crying. Tuma, long retired, had spent his life helping build the concrete edifices of power in Grozny. A construction engineer, he had worked on most of the government buildings that lined the center. In 1992, after the Soviet fall, when everything suddenly changed, he had dreams of his own construction firm, Tuma & Sons. War of course intervened. In the first campaign his house was leveled. Tuma had rebuilt it by hand. Then there had been plumbing, hot water even. Now there was only the outhouse and the well down the road.

"Never had such heat," Tuma repeated. He wandered beneath the tall walnut tree that dominated the yard. "There're so many grapes. And all dried up. We've never had such heat."

Timur brought Bislan. They had not always been good friends, but now they were bound for life. Together they had collected the bodies after the massacre. Together they had watched that night as the Russians returned, this time with trucks, big open flatbed trucks. They had watched as the soldiers returned to the houses that had not burned and emptied them of their belongings, of televisions and sofas, carpets and refrigerators. In the morning Bislan and Timor began to collect the bodies. Several they just put in the empty houses. They nailed the windows shut, so the dogs wouldn't get them. It took six days to find all the bodies.

Timur and Bislan spoke softly. They had had to tell what they had seen more than once already. They had had to tell it to the men who came here before me, the Russian "investigators." Men who carried video cameras and tape recorders. Men who showed no identification and did not give names. Men who were interested only in what the villagers knew.

As Bislan talked, Timur sat in a far corner of the yard. Hunched over, he stared at the rough ends of his short fingers. He was haunted by more than his memory of the massacre. Since the Fifth the Russians had come for him several times. Each time they took him away he came home with bruises. Only rarely did he interrupt Bislan.

"Forever," Timur said, when I asked if he would remember the commander's face. "A typical face, one of those simple Russian faces," he said. His men, too, he was sure were Russians, not Ossetians or Dagestanis or even Chechens, as some in Moscow had wanted me to believe.

EVEN BEFORE GOING to Chechnya, in Moscow and Nazran I had met survivors of the massacre. I sat and listened, often for hours, at times for days, as they told of the events of the Fifth. I took notes and wrote up the sessions, but these were not interviews. It was testimony.

In an empty hovel on Moscow's outskirts, where refugees from the Caucasus often lived, lying low from the Moscow police, I spent hours talking with Aset. She had risked arrest, or worse, and come to the capital to tell the human rights advocates what she had seen. I was to meet many others who had been in Aldy that day, but even years later I was convinced that Aset knew more about the massacre than anyone who had survived that day.

The first time we met she spoke in a breathless stream for nearly six hours. She had details on command, chronology in perfect place. She could quote her neighbors verbatim. She was, I feared, too good a witness. I worried that in her shock she had reconstructed the day in greater detail than she could possibly have known. I even entertained the idea that she might have been sent to Western human rights groups and Western correspondents to enhance the story of the massacre. But as I sat and listened to her talk not only of the massacre but of the war that preceded it and the war that had preceded that war, I came to believe her without pause, and I admired her courage. Given the prominent threat of retribution, only a handful of survivors had spoken publicly of the massacre. None spoke more eloquently than Aset. In the years that followed, we spoke often. I played and replayed the day as she saw it. Never once did she stray from her first telling. Never once did she retract or recast those first words.

To her the commander had been human. He had looked at her, she said, and nearly pleaded.

"What do you want me to do?" he asked as they stood together in the midst of the carnage. "My men shoot old men? Well, sometimes old men and young children carry things hidden on their bodies that blow up when you get too close. You know it yourself."

Aset did. She had seen others do it, and once the men had left that day, she, too, would tape a grenade to her waist. For two days she wore it hidden beneath her blouse.

"I told Timur I was worried about being raped," she said.

"Don't worry," her brother told her, "tape a grenade to your body, and if anyone comes at you, pull the plug."

Aset bought the grenade from a Russian soldier for four packs of Prima, the cheap Russian cigarettes that Shvedov, when he couldn't find his beloved *papirosi*, smoked.

Months later, after we had met countless times, Aset told me what her name meant. It was derived from Isis, she said, the Egyptian goddess. But Aset did not know what Isis had done. Isis had collected and reassembled the body of the murdered Osiris. Isis had impregnated herself from the corpse, becoming the goddess of the dead and funeral rites.

Aset's black hair hung sharply above her shoulders. Her eyes were deep-set and almond-shaped. Her cheekbones, high and round, were pronounced. Hers is hardly a typical Chechen face. Rarer still, for a woman in her fourth decade of life, Aset was single.

"The war," she said, when I asked why.

SHAMKHAN, THE MULLAH of Aldy, closed his eyes. He lifted his large hands and opened his pale palms to the sky. Every other man, including Issa, at the table did the same. The mullah led the prayer. He began: "*La ilaha illa allahu.* . . ." ("There is no God but Allah. . . .") In a moment, he drew his hands together and, with his eyes still closed, swept them down his broad face.

"I cannot speak of the events of February fifth," he said straight off. "I was not here. I left with the fighters on the night of January thirty-first."

Shamkhan was not a typical village mullah. Well over six feet and barrel-chested, he was slightly larger than a good-sized refrigerator. Moreover, he was impeccably dressed. Despite the high temperature, he was draped in a brocaded frockcoat. It was made of white cloth and lined with gold stitching. It lent Shamkhan a religious aura that impressed. So, too, did the staff of carved wood he carried in his hand. On his head he wore a heavy *papakha*, a tall gray hat of Astrakhan lamb's wool. I was hardly surprised, given his physique, to learn that Shamkhan had been, during his tour of duty in the Soviet Navy, the wrestling champion of the Black Sea Fleet.

He was the son of a mullah, but he came to the clergy "late," he said, in his mid-thirties. Shamkhan was born in Kazakhstan in 1953, the year Stalin died. He had been the mullah of Aldy since 1996–since the end of the first war. A graduate of Grozny's technical institute, before the war he worked as a welder in the Chechen gasworks.

"Gas or electric, I could do either, and I earned a lot. But after the death of my father my brothers wanted me to continue my education. So I entered the Islamic University here in 1992. I was about to complete my sixth year in the *Shari'a* department when the war started. And now two wars and still no degree."

Shvedov liked to remind Issa and me that before declaring their independence in 1991, Chechens were not the most observant Muslims. "Of all the peoples of the Caucasus," he said, "the Chechens were the last to find Islam." As with much of his ramblings, Shevdov's claim was at best half right. It was true that for decades a folk Islam, not a strict adherence to the laws of the Koran, had predominated among Chechens. It was also true that Dudayev, when he seized power in Grozny, had led a movement for independence first and for religious freedom second. The first chief justice of

Dudayev's *Shari'a* court smoked Marlboros during interviews. But as the first war raged, more and more young Chechen fighters donned green headbands that declared "Allah akbar" in Arabic. The Russian onslaught did what Dudayev had never envisioned: It turned the rebels ever more fundamentalist. By the time the second war began, the talk was less of independence and more of jihad.

THERE WAS A THEORY on why hell visited Aldy on February 5. It had to do with the brutality of Basayev and his comrade Khattab. I had heard it in Moscow from Russian journalists and in Nazran from Ingush bureaucrats. I heard it from Issa as well. It had to do with the abuses suffered after the end of the first war by the Russians who lived in Chernorechiye, the district bordering Aldy. It was once a workers' district, home to those who traded shifts at the nearby cement, chemical, and oil works. In Chernorechiye, the story went, the Russians enjoyed the best apartments. After the first war, once the Chechens had retaken Grozny, they exacted revenge. "That they kicked out Russians for apartments, this is absolutely true," said the reporter Andrei Babitsky. "It happened everywhere in Grozny, but Chernorechiye had a large Russian population. And in the months before the second war, the practice there is said to have grown more and more violent, with Russians leaving their apartments through their windows."

Chernorechiye suffered a *zachistka* the same day as Aldy. The theory held that the Russians who had come on the Fifth had come to avenge the Russians killed in Chernorechiye. "WE HAVE RETURNED," read graffito painted in large letters during the *zachistka* in Chernorechiye, "YOUR VILLAGE NEIGHBORS."

There was another theory, one that concerned the question of fighters. In the wake of the Aldy massacre, news stories and human rights reports downplayed the possibility that Chechen fighters had been in Aldy. But the fighters had been there. Babitsky had been there with them. On January 14, in his last radio broadcast from Grozny before disappearing, Babitsky told Radio Liberty's Russian listeners, "In the village of Aldy, where I was also today with armed Chechens, bombs and missiles hit literally two hundred to two hundred and fifty meters from us." The fighters had come through the village, Aset said. Some had stayed a few days, only to rest and have her treat their wounds. The nearest rebel base, everyone insisted, had been in the adjoining district, District 20, three bus stops east from Aset's house.

Babitsky, when I asked him later what he had seen in Aldy during his hellish last weeks in Grozny, was forthcoming. "I was in Aldy nearly every day. In the middle of January I did spend two days there at my close friend's house." His friend, Babitsky said, was Kazbek, the commander of Aldy. "I'd thought Kazbek had surely died, but he survived the *zachistka*. He'd dug a hole in his cellar so deep that even though the Russians threw a grenade in, he lived."

Aldy, however, was never a rebel stronghold. The fighters were too smart to stay for long. Chernorechiye, Babitsky and other reporters who had been going to Chechnya since the first war told me, was by far the better defensive position. Chernorechiye sat high above the road and, unlike Aldy, boasted multistory buildings. For the wounded, Aldy offered a sanctuary, a rare corner of Grozny where there were still people, good water, and, most of all, medicine. But given the number of villagers who remained in Aldy, the fighters were reluctant to use it as a position. The fighters, Babitsky said, deemed the village too important to risk the inevitable reprisal. "They thought," he said, "Aldy was a good refuge."

THE CARNAGE THAT DESTROYED so much of Aldy is not peculiar to our time. Indeed Aldy, unbeknownst to the Russians who arrived on February 5, had a history. A river of violence and sadness found its source there in the eighteenth century, during the reign of Catherine the Great. In 1785 one of the first battles between Chechens and Russians took place when Catherine ordered her troops to storm Aldy, the village that at the time spanned the area of modern-day Aldy and Chernorechiye.

Catherine chose the target with purpose. Long before Yermolov built the line of forts that began with Grozny, Peter the Great had built the Line, a Great Wall of Russian forts and Cossack stánitsas. By 1784 the Russians had finished their critical garrison in the North Caucasus, the fort at Vladikavkaz. But in the following year Catherine's men suffered an unprecedented defeat on the Sunzha River—at the hands of the followers of a mysterious Chechen holy warrior.

In 1785, Prince Grigori Potemkin—Catherine's viceroy in the Caucasus and the favorite among her lovers—learned of a potent force emerging from

Aldy, a resistance movement led by a shepherd. Potemkin heard the news from his cousin Major-General Pavel Potemkin, who sent an alarming communiqué from the field: "On the opposite bank of the river Sunzha in the village of Aldy, a prophet has appeared and started to preach. He has submitted superstitious and ignorant people to his will by claiming to have had a revelation."[35]

Many believe that Imam Shamil, the holy warrior who led the longest resistance to the tsar, was the first great Chechen fighter. He was not. The title belongs to Sheikh Mansour. (Shamil, an Avar from Dagestan, was not even Chechen. Sheikh Mansour was.) History tells Mansour's story variously. His genealogy, theology, even name, have never been definitively revealed. But in the Caucasus what motivates men and triggers their weapons is not reality, but a perception of reality. In the realm of perceived reality, Mansour is revered as the first in the long line of Chechen holy warriors. He was born a peasant named Ushurma in Aldy. He had the good fortune to come of age just in time for Russia's southern onslaught.

"Muhammad paid this simple peasant a visit," Shamkhan told me. "He revealed himself to this young man because he was the purest of believers. The time had come, the prophet told him, to lead a *Ghazavat* on the Russians."

In 1783, Ushurma took the name Mansour–"conqueror" in Arabic–and later added the honorific "sheikh." A devout believer in Sufism, a mystical strain of Islam, Mansour already had a following. Sheikh Mansour led the Naqshbandi Tariqa, or path of belief.

Eager to please the empress, his lover and lord, Prince Potemkin dispatched three thousand troops to capture Mansour. They stormed Aldy but did not find him. Frustrated, they torched the village. Mansour's men got their revenge. They ambushed the Russians in the nearby woods and killed, the chronicles attest, more than six hundred men. Potemkin had to tell Catherine that nearly half his force had been lost. Many had drowned, trying to flee, in the Sunzha's muddy waters. An "unfortunate occurrence," Prince Potemkin called it in his report to Catherine.[36] The blood feud had begun.

As Catherine's men routed his followers, Mansour took refuge in the Ottoman fortress of Anapa. In 1791 he was captured and shipped off to St. Petersburg, where he spent his last years in the Schlüsselberg Fortress, an island prison in the Neva River near Lake Ladoga.[37] But Mansour's spirit never left Chechnya. In Aldy it was especially strong.

"We all know the history of this village. Sheikh Mansour lives on in each of us," the mullah Shamkhan said, leaning forward on his staff. "We feel his strength every day. We know the struggle began here." Shamkhan had just come from leading a service for one of the *shaheed*, the martyrs of the Fifth of February. At the service, dancing the *zikr*, a religious dance, was Magomed Dolkaev, an elegant elder with a flowing white beard who claimed Sheikh Mansour as an ancestor. No one knew the true genealogy. But as Shamkhan told me, it was not important.

A year and a half later Dolkaev was dead. He, too, had fallen victim to the new times—shot four times in the head by an unknown gunman in his home in Aldy.

ISSA, WHO SAT IN silence as I listened to Shamkhan, could no longer hold his peace. He had observed it all, taking in the mullah and his story with the weary eyes of a crocodile. When he begged permission to interrupt, I consented with a shrug to the inevitable.

Issa leaned forward, squaring his elbows on the table across from the mullah, with a question. "How come Maskhadov," he said, referring to the military commander elected Chechnya's president after the first war, "couldn't build a state that could defend any citizen, no matter his faith?"

His voice had lost its usual calm and was rising. "Where were all these brave fighters when there was not one Russian soldier here? When all you had to do was bury one, or two, or three bandits so that none of this would have happened?"

Shamkhan invoked the name of Allah. He swore that he was "against any embodiment of evil," that he could not "tolerate Wahhabism," and was a foe of "any extremism."

Issa did not let up.

"You say you left with the fighters. Abandoned the village during the siege. You and I speak the same language. Tell me, as the spiritual father of these people, how did we come to this? How can we live like this?"

Shamkhan struggled for a rejoinder. He stiffened his broad back and condemned the plagues that had visited Chechnya since the Soviet fall: the militarism of Dudayev, the romanticism of Maskhadov, the banditry of Basayev, the foreign Wahhabi virus of Khattab, and the venal hunger of the rest of Chechnya's warlords. "All this we have earned," he said, "because of our ignorance. Thanks to our lack of enlightenment, we were unable to establish any order."

The mullah was talking to Issa but looking at me. He said he had never led anyone to any jihad. He said the fighters had wanted to take him earlier from Aldy, that they were afraid the Russians would kill him on sight. He swore to Allah that everything he had done was done not in the name of Dudayev or Maskhadov or Basayev or Khattab, but in the name of Allah and Allah alone.

As the torrent of words poured forth, I realized Shamkhan was talking too much. Then, suddenly, he dropped his guard. He declared his conscience clean. He said he had done all that had been asked of him, that he had journeyed "the path from beginning to end," the path that was "written in blood."

Shamkhan, I realized then, had been with Basayev and the fighters the night they broke through the siege of Grozny. "The path" was the fighters' macabre retreat through the minefields to Alkhan-Kala.

I pressed for details.

"They needed someone to bless and bury the dead," he said. "So I made this journey with them and with my own eyes saw how they died. If someone were to sit and tell me what they had seen along this path, I swear to Allah, I would never believe him. I would not believe people could die like that."

The fighters had taken him from Aldy on the last day of January. Before he left, the mullah told his followers to stay in the village. "Do not abandon your homes to the Russians," he had said. The words, as Shamkhan recalled them, weighed heavily.

The minefields killed hundreds during the fighters' retreat. Others froze to death. He had stayed with the fighters for the entire trek, from Grozny to the snowbound mountains in the south. He had left the fighters in their mountain hideaways.

Would they fight until the end? I asked.

"What lies in their hearts," Shamkhan said, "is to me a dark wood."

TEN

THE CREEK WAS DARK green and cloudy. As Issa and I bathed in it, resting our hands on the sludgy rocks below, our feet and arms stirred the water the color of burned sugar. Issa was telling me tales of the glory of his youth in Grozny, but I was preoccupied. I was wondering what else lay in the mucky creek of Shali.

We walked here together, through the nettles of the overgrown orchard that was the backyard of the small house where Issa's mother and two sisters lived. His mother was eighty; his sisters were in their fifties. Throughout the years of war, Shali, lying in the plains just south of Grozny, had been spared the wholesale destruction of the capital and nearly every other town and village in Chechnya. Issa's mother and sisters lived here throughout the shelling, the bombings, and the military sweeps.

Inside the house it was dark and cool. There were two rooms and a kitchen. Issa did not say it, but the house was all he had in Chechnya now. Once he had a comfortable apartment in Grozny, but it was lost to the first war. He managed to save some of the furniture–a gold-rimmed mirror, a lacquered table, a velvety divan–vestiges of the Chechen elite of the Soviet era that now sat like islands in the biggest room of the house. Except for the salvaged treasures, the house was empty. The second room was filled with rolled-up carpets and chairs stacked against a wall, more remnants of a lost life.

The creek, no matter what toxins of war lay in its waters, was cooling. Like the children who jumped into it, we were naked to our underwear. Our shirts and trousers, stiffened with dirt and road dust, hung from a low cherry tree that twisted above the muddy bank. One side of the creek was lined by the overgrown yards. The other was a steep bank the children used as a diving platform. Behind them were only empty fields. The children leaped in, hands over knees, shouting as they fell through the air.

In the evening, after we dried ourselves with worn hand towels and dressed again in the same clothes, Issa's mother, Sabiat, took me on a tour. She was so thin and her back so bent that it was remarkable she could walk, let alone cook and clean. "We have everything here," she said, pointing to the trees that stood amid the weeds: "Apricot, pear, apple, cherry." The heat of the afternoon brought the smell of the fruit close. Sabiat squinted at the cloudless sky. "Why?" she asked. She needed no more words; she meant the war. "Somebody must want it," she said.

Everywhere there was greenery. Vines climbed high along the back wall. On a tall wooden fence, roses, pink and red, bloomed. The garden, Issa's mother said, was all she needed now. Nothing more. "But the fruit of the trees," said Issa's younger sister, "is not as good since the war." She was called Zulei, and her elder sister Zura.

The courtyard, the summer living room of houses across Chechnya, was clean and quiet. Here the routine of the day unfolded. In the morning the sisters washed clothes in metal basins. In the afternoon their mother fried potatoes and boiled lamb. And in the evening Shvedov lounged on a faded threadbare couch that sat in the middle of the narrow porch. Above the porch, in the corners of its slanting roof, swallows nested.

"Our mama's life has been a hard one," Zura said.

"Mama," Issa commanded, "tell him about the deportation."

There was no need, and he knew that. The deportation was not history. It informed the daily conversation in Chechnya. Issa's mother had been twenty-two in 1944. She remembered clearly how the NKVD soldiers had herded them into the freight cars—in all, more than fourteen thousand cars were needed—and sent them off to the remote Soviet republics of Central Asia. Along with hundreds of thousands of Chechens and Ingush, Sabiat survived thirteen years in Central Asia. Exile was hard, of course, she said. But it was better, much better, than this war. "They gave us a small plot of land and a little house. We could grow a garden."

Tired of talk, Sabiat went back to her chores. In her slippers and a flowered cotton dress, she reached for a short brush, a dozen switches tied to a stick. She was intent on sweeping the dirt from the concrete of her courtyard. She stooped low and, despite the heat, worked the brush with purpose and without pause.

"Every night and every morning our mama cleans," Zulei said. "Only the water from the well will she let us get ourselves."

She had survived Central Asia, the road back to Grozny in 1957, and the loss of her husband, to a car accident years ago that came on the Prophet's birthday. "She must work or else . . . ," said her daughter Zura.

As Issa's mother swept, Shvedov stubbed out another *papirosa* in the tin coffee can on the sofa. After he got up slowly from the old couch and disappeared into the coolness of the house, Sabrat continued to sweep. A month later Issa would call and tell me that his mother's heart had at last given out.

ELEVEN

ILYAS CAME TO SEE me after dark. Darkness unnerved the Russian soldiers in Chechnya but liberated the locals.

"Why do they say," he asked, "that every journalist who comes here now is a spy?" Ilyas was a fighter and not afraid to probe. Chechens are, without effort, obsessed with spies. Cultural legends and historical mythologizing were one thing, but in Chechnya there was a veritable industry in conspiracy theories. The war was not Moscow's fault alone. Washington, Wall Street, world Zionism had also colluded against the Chechens. Intelligence agencies—the CIA, Mossad, MI6—loomed large everywhere. The plots and subplots were infinite but followed one story line. "They have hijacked our fight for freedom," Ilyas said, "in a global geostrategic fight for our oil."

The worst culprits of course were the journalists. In the Zone every reporter was a fifth columnist in poor disguise. Sitting with Ilyas, I was not in a particularly comfortable position. (At the time Issa had announced with unsettling confidence that he thought I was the only foreign correspondent in Chechnya.) I had never worked with Fred Cuny, the Texan genius of emergency relief, who had been killed in Chechnya in 1996. But I knew well several people who had. They remained convinced Cuny had been killed by Chechens acting at the behest of the Russian security service. Moreover, every day I was made amply aware of the price tag on any foreigner's head in these parts.

Ilyas lived in Urus-Martan, the third-largest town in Chechnya and a place known as a center of the new Wahhabism. He agreed to meet in Gudermes, in an apartment with little furniture and less light, one short block from the Russian military headquarters. Although he moved about the city freely and was unafraid to meet a foreign correspondent, Ilyas said it was better to meet at night.

ANDREW MEIER

At first we sat in silence. I tried a few entreaties without luck. Ilyas was short and stocky, with wavy hair that curled long behind his ears. A reddish brown beard was coming onto his square cheeks. Failing to engage him in small talk—where he was from ("here and there"), what he did ("this and that")—I decided to up the ante.

"Why do they call you an *amir*?" I asked.

"Because I lead a group, a group of fighters."

I had heard the term *amir* before. In Afghanistan, in the summer of 1996, weeks before the Taliban took Kabul, their leaders in Kandahar spoke reverently of their *amir*, their leader, the one-eyed mullah Muhammad Omar who had taken to calling himself the *Amir ul Momineen*, Commander of the Faithful. When I met Ahmed Shah Massoud, the military genius who stood behind the Afghan government then clinging to Kabul, Massoud spit the term out.

"No one can call himself the *amir*," Massoud said. "It is sacrilege to all Muslims."

In Chechnya being an *amir* meant Ilyas had gone Wahhabi. "Wahhabism," at least in Chechnya, is an imprecise term. Religiously, it could mean nearly anything. Yet militarily, its meaning was clear: It meant Ilyas had joined Jama'at, the fighting arm of the would-be Islamic fundamentalists who were now claiming recruits across Chechnya—even in Gudermes, the Russians' administrative center. Being an *amir* meant that Ilyas, though scarcely twenty years old, controlled six fighters, who, as he put it, "would do anything I ask."

"The Wahhabis," Ilyas explained, "are anyone who believes in the need to cleanse our nation and who will sacrifice himself in the jihad against Russia," and, he politely added, "against the United States and its allies as well."

In Kandahar that summer of 1996 the Taliban had convened a gathering of mullahs, one of the largest ever. In the dark of night, their high-pitched prayers woke me. I had never heard a more terrifying sound. To me, their cries did not ring of piety, but of a dark passion laced with bloodlust. Later I told a UN worker, a gentle Somalian who had survived the worst of Mogadishu, what I had heard. The Somalian pulled me aside and whispered: "You have heard the sound of evil. You may think me paranoid, but these Talibs are dangerous. They will only grow and foster more evil. You

80

must warn your government, tell them not to support them. They will take this country and turn it into the world's terrorist camp."

In Putin's War, Kremlin aides and Russian generals had grown fond of spinning tales of "thousands of Taliban fighters" flooding into Chechnya to aid their brothers. Although the Chechens had boasted of the aid their Islamic brothers had provided, chiefly mercenaries and money, the ties among the Chechen rebels and the Taliban and Al Qaeda were shadowy. So as we sat across a small table, cupping our hands around thin glasses of tea, I asked Ilyas if he could refute Russia's claims.

"It's nonsense," he said. "We have no Taliban here. Did we have Arabs fighting on our side? Yes. But a hundred or two at most. Do we support the Taliban? Of course. They are our spiritual brothers. They, too, are fighting to purify Islam and liberate it from its oppressors."

As we sat together in that corner of Chechnya, the horror of September 11, 2001, lay a year in the future. But the Kremlin had long emphasized reports of Khattab's ties to bin Laden.

"Khattab is our *amir,*" Ilyas said. "He is a man of great purity who knows how to bring *Shari'a* to our land." But as pro-Chechen Web sites had long made obvious in numerous languages, the Black Arab's expertise was not restricted to religion. An adept commander, Khattab had become renowned as the mastermind of one of the first war's deadliest ambushes. Russian and Western intelligence agencies also considered Khattab an able fund raiser, reaping financial support, if not large numbers of mercenaries, from Islamic radicals around the world.[38]

"New money comes every week," Ilyas boasted, refusing to name the country or organization of its origin. "For this we can thank Khattab as well." Ilyas did not disguise the fact that some of his fellow Wahhabi fighters had come from Saudi Arabia and elsewhere across the Arab world, but the majority, he insisted, were Chechens. And their arms, he added, were Russian. Russian officers and soldiers were more than willing, for a price, to keep the enemy well armed.

Ilyas had clear ideas about the future, his own and his people's. As we sat in the dank apartment in Gudermes, and scattered gunfire pierced the night air outside, he laid out for me—in far more detail than I felt safe knowing—the fighters' plans. I pulled out my well-worn map of Chechnya and spread it on the thin carpet. Ilyas's eyes danced. In Soviet times such maps were restricted to government eyes. I'd bought it from a street vendor in Moscow, a block from the Lubyanka. But like many fighters, Ilyas had never seen a map of his land.

Excited, he charted, town by town, gorge by gorge, where the resistance forces now bided their time. He traced the roads in and around Grozny. He knew where each curve and hill lay. His voice quickened as he talked of the rebel leaders Basayev and Khattab, and the lesser field commanders now spread across Chechnya. His fingers danced over the map as he shared his best estimates of how many men each commander controlled. Tasks differed, he said, from assassination to suicide bombing to intelligence, but one mission united the fighters: to carry the war on, to keep the occupiers in a vise, to ensure they suffer a slow, but constant, loss of life.

"We have no other choice," he said when I asked why he had chosen the Wahhabi path. "Once we believed our elders. We believed it when they told us moral virtue would bring victory. But we are a new force, and we know we must purify the soul of our nation. Today. Before it is too late."

Ilyas was educated, intelligent, and impatient. He wore a Swiss mountaineering watch, a state-of-the-art piece that boasted a digital compass, a barometer, and an altitude gauge. He had a clear sense that the struggle would be long, perhaps even without end. Yet he was convinced it was just. Fighting the Russians, he said, was the only way for a morally pure Chechen man to live and the most righteous way to die. Ilyas was not a big fighter, just one of thousands in the new scaled-down resistance. Small teams, young, well armed, and dedicated to the *ghazavat*, were now forming to run sabotage and reconnaissance missions. They would take out Russian soldiers in the markets. They would take out Chechen traitors in their sleep. They would blow up checkpoints. They would ambush convoys at will.

I had seen Ilyas's handiwork up close. That afternoon, as Issa, Shvedov, Yura, and I were making our way from Grozny to Gudermes, four agitated young Russian soldiers bade us stop at their checkpoint near the town of Djalka, just ten miles from Grozny. At first we thought another convoy was coming and we would have to let it pass. But when I got out of the UAZik, I saw that was not the case. Half a mile or so beyond the checkpoint, in the dense woods that divided two brown fields, a firefight raged. I could hear the exchange of automatic rifle fire and, through the shafts of billowing smoke, see a trio of helicopters swoop down and fire into the woods. The Russian soldiers, suntanned OMON officers from Irkutsk, checked our documents. Shvedov asked what had happened. They shrugged their shoulders.

"Something," one said.

"Nothing," said the other.

They would not let us through, so we stood at the checkpoint and watched the spectacle.

After half an hour a bus that had crossed through the firefight approached. Issa went to talk to its driver.

"It's the train," he said when he returned. His wan smile revealed delight.

The Russians had recently started running trains again between Gudermes to Grozny to supply their headquarters with food, fuel, and weapons.

"They hit the train," Issa explained.

As more cars joined the line behind us, Issa talked to the drivers. No matter where we went in Chechnya, Issa seemed to know everyone and everyone knew him. It was not always a comforting equation. He returned with details: guerrillas in the woods, remote-controlled bombs on the tracks, an armored car with a cache of Russian weapons blown up. "It will soon be over," Issa announced, with the confidence of a man who had grown used to the timetable of guerrilla warfare. He was right. In an hour we were back in Gudermes, and several hours later I was sitting with Ilyas.

"You saw the remains of the train, didn't you?" Ilyas asked. We had been going over the map when he paused an index finger on Djalka. "You must have been there when the train was hit this afternoon, no?" he asked, revealing a knowledge of both the attack and my whereabouts. It was a polite way of letting me know that his group had helped bomb the train. The ambush was effective. The train was hauling two carloads of soldiers and several wagons of matériel to Khankala, the Russian military headquarters at Grozny's eastern edge, when four remote-controlled bombs exploded in succession. Six soldiers were wounded, and one woman, a cook, was killed. The train ground to a stop. The soldiers walked the ten miles to Khankala on foot and in fear.

"We will not give up," Ilyas said. "We will hit them in small ways, but every day. Some colonel gets up to go to work, ties his shoes, puts on his coat, starts his car, and he is gone."

Given the frequency of assassinations in Chechnya, I knew this was not a rhetorical flourish. In fact, as we spoke, another squad was moving through the darkness toward its target. In the early morning, a quiet Sunday in the town of Alkhan-Yurt, the town's Chechen administrator, accused of serving the occupiers, was to be assassinated outside his home, shot by more than a dozen bullets.[39]

"When will it end?" I asked.

"When they leave."

Like many Chechens, Ilyas did not refer to the Russian soldiers in their midst as anything but "they."

As our talk stretched into its third hour, I sensed that if there were enough young men in Chechnya like Ilyas, the Russians might succeed in bringing a semblance of governance to the region but would never again rest comfortably as its guardians.

The hatred, Ilyas assured me, would always burn. A group of young men in Urus-Martan were now back in school, learning how to blow themselves up. The suicide bombers, he said, were not mentally disturbed, drug-addicted, or eager to earn money for their families, all motives the Kremlin had provided reporters in Moscow. They were Chechens, he said, who had been through the so-called filtration camps, the jails the Russians had established in the republic since the days of the first war, ostensibly to weed out terrorists from civilian men. The filtration camps were notorious locales for torture.[40]

"They ram steel rods into your anus until they nearly kill you," Ilyas said. "It would be better to be killed, because you come back to us humiliated. For a Chechen man there is only one thing to do: avenge."

As the kettle boiled a second time, Ilyas fell silent. Then he raised his eyes and bore them into mine. "Are you a Christian?" he asked.

"No," I said. "I am a Jew."

"So you're an American, a journalist, and a Jew. Are you not scared?"

It seemed as much a warning as a question. I said, banally, that for years, ever since I had first heard of the Chechens, back in 1989, when my friend and host in Moscow Andrei had laughed at the Chechens' first stirrings for sovereignty, I had dreamed of coming to Chechnya.

Ilyas did not allow his eyes to drift. He only tightened his dark brows. "But you have no fear?"

I mumbled something about the nature of journalism in the modern world, how you had to measure risks and walk appropriately, how you never knew, of course, but you set your itineraries with care and trusted your judgment. Ilyas did not nod or smile. He kept on staring. I said no more. But as the panic began to pull at my neck and the breath in my lungs tightened, I wanted to tell him, "Yes, yes, you raise a good point. A great point. I am in fact scared out of my mind."

TWELVE

IN THE YEARS SINCE the first Russian onslaught in 1994, the kidnapping industry replaced petroleum crude as the primary contributor to Chechnya's gross domestic product. No full tally exists, but by the best estimates, several thousand people fell prey to the trade in hostages. Reporters, technical advisers, and aid workers were among those kidnapped. Anyone of course was a target, but by far the majority of those "stolen," as the Chechens put it, were natives of the Caucasus: Chechens, Dagestanis, Ingush, Georgians, Armenians. Things had gotten particularly bad of late.

"Kidnapping's the only business that works in Chechnya," Shvedov announced one night as we dined on boiled potatoes and fatty squares of boiled lamb. We sat beneath a dying moon in the yard of Issa's mother's house in Shali. We listened to bullfrogs croaking in the creek and nightingales shrilling in the trees.

"Strange," Issa said, "the nightingales are still here."

Shvedov lit a *papirosa* and spun the dial on his transistor to Radio Free Chechnya, the station Moscow had launched days earlier to enlighten the Chechens. The voice of General Troshev filled the courtyard. He was promising his interlocutor, an army press aide, that from now on "every human right" would be respected during *zachistka* operations. Every so often a thunderclap of artillery guns buckled through the air. The Russians were outside Shali, aiming at targets a few miles from the house. The shelling punctuated the talk of kidnapping.

"Don't you worry about someone stealing us from here?" Shvedov asked Issa.

The thought had crossed my mind. I was not the first journalist to stay in his mother's house. The word was certainly out.

"If they want you," Issa answered, "they can get anywhere."

Issa knew a lot about the kidnapping industry. For months he had tried to secure the release of an Armenian teenager kidnapped in Moscow and now held near Vedeno, the town that anchors Chechnya's southeastern corner. ("A favor of the heart," he explained.) The boy, he said, was the son of an old comrade from his oil-drilling days in Siberia. Wherever we traveled, Issa was in deep negotiations to get the boy back. "That Armenian kid is keeping me going," he said. He meant his fight to save the boy's life. But I had heard another motive, the fifty-thousand-dollar share of the ransom Issa would get for bringing the boy to his father alive.

The trade in humans, and their remains, brought all the players in the Zone to the table. There were the Islamic wise men: the mufti of Vedeno, a slight fellow with a stiff manner and a beard that seemed too well trimmed, and his taller, quieter cohort, the mufti of Elistanzhi. One's eyes never stopped smiling, the other's were cold. (They both made my skin crawl.) Then there were the Jama'at fighters, young men like Ilyas with grand ambitions and the first signs of facial hair. And the local FSB, the men from Russia's security service. "Necessary intermediaries" Issa called them.

A few nights later Issa and I lay on opposite sofas in the big empty room in the house in Shali, trying to get to sleep. It was too hot to cover oneself with anything. I had rolled my dirty jeans into a pillow. In the darkness Issa continued to talk. He had been sullen all day. The deal for the Armenian had gone south. The boy was dead, killed some time ago. The body, he said, might even be impossible to retrieve. "How do I tell his father?" Issa asked. He was struggling, it seemed, less for an answer than for a way to accept the revenue loss.

KIDNAPPING WAS ONLY the most notorious plague bred in the years that followed the first war. The interregnum, above all, had yielded a dismally poor effort at self-rule. Perhaps the urge for revenge was too great, or the desire for personal power too strong, but the Chechens, the would-be victors of the first war, proved unable to win the peace.

A few months after I received the video from Aldy, the villagers' desperate attempt to send word of the massacre to the outside, I got a second video from Chechnya. This one did not feature Chechens butchered by Russians. It featured a Chechen killed by Chechens. In Kandahar in 1996 I had heard tales of public executions, of adulterers stoned to death. In the interregnum the Chechens did not establish the Taliban's vice squad, the Committee for the Prevention of Vice and the Promotion of Virtue. But they did mete out *Shari'a* in its bloodiest form.

During Putin's War the Russian Interior Ministry got smart. They culled all the snippets of video they could find that testified to the abuse—kidnapping, starvation, head and finger chopping—suffered by Russians and foreigners at the alleged hands of Chechens. The ministry then invited reporters to come view their snuff films. Not eager to savor the barbarism, I declined.

This second tape would have better served the ministry's purpose. It offered a scene from a *Shari'a* court, in early August 1996, on the day before the Chechens retook Grozny. Five Chechen fighters sit in a bright wood, their legs crossed on a blanket spread on the grass. The bearded man seated in the middle is Basayev, the most famous of the fighters. Across from them stands an older man, gray-haired. He is tall and frail. His hands are tied behind his back, and a bandage is wrapped around his forehead, but the old man does not cower. The dialogue is ruthless and revealing. Basayev, for the sake of the camera, interrogates the old man.

BASAYEV: *Acting what?*
OLD MAN: *Acting head of administration.*
BASAYEV: *Whose head?*
OLD MAN: *The region's.*
BASAYEV: *Who put you in that job?*
OLD MAN: *Bugayev. Koshman recommended it, gave him the paper. He signed it and gave it to him.*

BASAYEV: *And who are they? Who's this Koshman?*

OLD MAN: *The head of the government.*

BASAYEV: *Of what?*

OLD MAN: *The Chechen republic.*

BASAYEV: *Oh, I see. That makes you a national traitor. Know that?*

OLD MAN: *I never was. And am not now.*

BASAYEV: *Yes, you are, you're a traitor. You've been afraid since '93 that the Russians wouldn't come. Ever since you stood on the Theater Square [in Grozny]. Now you say you're the prefect of the Vedeno region.*

OLD MAN: *I am the acting head.*

BASAYEV: *Makes no difference to me. It was you pigs who brought this misery to our people.*

OLD MAN: *When you are done, I will explain.*

BASAYEV: *I am done.*

OLD MAN: *The people, when they stood on the Theater Square, said that the Russian troops were coming. We had to come together so they couldn't enter. We had to prevent this tragedy. And we all stood there with economic demands.*

BASAYEV: *Don't give me propaganda. Better you tell me why you sold out to the Russians.*

OLD MAN: *I swear, I brought no one any misery, and I never sold out to any Russians.*

BASAYEV: *You're just working for them?*

OLD MAN: *I am not working for them. I am a teacher. I taught our Chechen children.*

BASAYEV: *How is it you never worked for them? Who is this Koshman?*

OLD MAN: *Chairman of the government of the Chechen republic.*

BASAYEV: *Which republic? Where is the Chechen republic? You let in these Russians, pushed them forward, leading the people to this misery.*

OLD MAN: *Not because of me.*

BASAYEV: *That's what you say—"not because of me"? So who destroyed this land?*

OLD MAN: *Those who have sinned, they are the sinners.*

BASAYEV: *God will judge, is that it?*

OLD MAN: *He will judge. Soon we shall know.*[41]

Basayev flattens a piece of paper on the blanket spread across the grass. He takes out a rubber stamp and, after warming it with his breath, stamps the paper sharply. Then, switching into Russian to lend his voice an air of state authority, he reads the death sentence: "The military field court of the Central Front of the Armed Forces of the Chechen Republic of Ichkeria, for crimes against the state and the Chechen people, committed under aggravating circumstances, resulting in numerous victims among the population and the barbaric violation of the Chechen Republic of Ichkeria, in accordance with Article 50: 'Violation of the Constitutional Order'; Article 51, Part A and B: 'Inciting War against the State'; Article 52: 'Collaboration with Enemy States'; Article 53: 'Espionage against the Country' of Chapter Five of the Criminal Code of the Chechen Republic of Ichkeria, all of these qualifying as a crime against the state sentences Zakayev, Amir Abdullakhavich, born in the year 1940, living on Veterinarian Street, House 4, village of Dyshnee Vedeno, Vedeno Region, to the highest form of punishment, execution. The sentence is final and not subject to appeal."

Zakayev stands against a broad tree. His hands remain tied. He does not flinch.

"Bear witness that you are a Muslim," a voice offscreen says.

As shots ring out, the camera lurches close. A ribbon of automatic fire cuts through the air. The old man's knees buckle as he falls to the ground.

"Maybe after burning in hell, you'll end up in heaven," the voice says, "*inshallah*."

The execution appeared in a video made by pro-Russian Chechens. Issa had provided the narration. The scene seemed staged and, given the source, a potential fake. I showed it to a number of Chechens in Moscow who doubted its authenticity. Then I showed it to Adam, a former Chechen fighter, once an associate of Basayev's. Adam had long ago put down his gun and taken to working as a fixer, getting foreign reporters in and out of Chechnya. He recognized the scene. It was not an interrogation, Adam said, but "a trial." "Some teacher," he said of the man executed. "A son of a bitch. He worked for the Russians."

Chechens everywhere told me the same thing: that the worst were the enemies within, the Chechens who crossed to the Russian side. They were the ones, they said, who had brought the nation to its knees and now threatened to cut out its heart.

"Men like this old man were not innocents," Adam said when I stopped the videotape. "They were traitors. Not enough of them were killed."

THIRTEEN

THE RUSSIANS, I HAD come to believe, had convinced themselves they needed only one ally to win hearts and minds in Chechnya. The decimation of the Chechen people and the destruction of their homes could do only so much. To establish a lasting rule, as General Troshev proclaimed more than once, Moscow would have to rely on the Good Chechen. In Raibek Tovzayev, they imagined they found one.

"Salaam aleikum," I said, extending my hand. "Peace to you."

"Va aleikum salaam," Raibek said in the customary return. "Come in peace."

Raibek was a muscled man with unshorn silvering hair and clear blue eyes. He was eager to show me his ID, a Russian military pass encased in red leather. It declared him deputy chief of the administration of his native Vedeno region, not only Chechnya's most fabled corner but its most strategic as well. General Troshev had put Raibek on retainer, made him a free lance in the employ of the Russian military. His men, some one hundred irregulars who in times of peace tended fat cows and thin goats, were now fed, uniformed, and armed on Troshev's budget. Raibek's task was daunting: to secure Vedeno for the Russians and make a good show, at the very least, of keeping its peace.

In Putin's War, Troshev had long spoken passionately of the new, "humane" plan. Raised in Grozny, the general considered himself a native, someone who appreciated Chechen traditions. Moscow, Troshev assured viewers in nightly appearances on Russian television, would not make the same mistakes twice. This time the generals would meet with the *Shura*, the local council of elders, in each town and convince them of the need to cleanse their land of "illegal bandit formations." Chechens would rush to Moscow's side, Troshev reasoned, for they, too, hated the terrorists and bandits, kidnappers, and cutthroats. Troshev struck a historic echo: "the good Chechen" had been the elusive ideal of his nineteenth-century forebear General Yermolov.

Raibek's attraction had little to do with loyalty to the federal cause—he professed an undisguised disdain for it—and everything to do with geography and history. His fiefdom spanning a ridge above the Vedeno Gorge was the best line of defense against Basayev and Khattab, who had retreated to the forbidding hills to the east, the Nozhai Yurt region. The Russians also liked Raibek's history. A native of the village of Pervomaiskoye, which overlooks Vedeno, Raibek had known Basayev since both were small children, and it was no secret, in Grozny and in Moscow, that Raibek and the most wanted man in Russia were mortal enemies.

It was not easy to visit Raibek. We left Shali just after dawn and followed a well-worn road south through the pink haze of the midsummer sunrise. Layers of mist clung to the brown fields at the foot of the mountains. After a series of checkpoints we came to the mouth of the Vedeno Gorge, a deep ravine of rock cut by centuries of snow melting from the Caucasian massifs. As we headed south, the black mountains rose ever higher around us.

Vedeno, centered in the depths of the ravine, had long loomed as the vortex of the war. Once the home of Imam Shamil, it was now renowned as the birthplace and base of his namesake Basayev. Here, in the 1990s, Basayev rekindled the legend of the nineteenth-century Shamil to rally his compatriots against their Slavic masters. Now Vedeno was the dark crossroads where seemingly incompatible forces met, the kidnapping industry flourished, and firefights flared easily. More than any other town in Chechnya, it was saturated with young men who carried plenty of ammunition and few loyalties. "Vedeno is the key," Ilyas, the would-be Wahhabi, told me. "Vedeno is the heart of the new Islam. From there the cleansing of our nation will come." It was also considered, by many Chechens and Russians alike, the heart of the conflict. From here the road south leads through the mountains to Georgia. For the fighters, it had become a vital supply line. "Whoever wins Vedeno," Ilyas said, "wins the war." It was a prophecy I heard again and again.

"YOU'LL LOVE RAIBEK," Issa told me as the UAZik slipped up the steep gravel road to his mountain redoubt, "because he's a modern-day Hadji Murad." Tolstoy had first heard the tale of Hadji Murad as a young man in the 1850s, when he lived among the tsarist troops in a Cossack stanitsa in Chechnya's northern plains. It is the story of a famed Chechen warrior who, facing death at the hands of his former ally Shamil, goes over to the Russians. But Murad, as I reminded Issa, does not end up well. He escapes from

ANDREW MEIER

the Russians, hoping to free his family from Shamil, but is killed by bounty hunters—Russian, Cossack, and Chechen—eager to claim the price on his head. The tale turns tragic as a Cossack delivers Murad's severed head to the Russians who once praised his strong will and gentlemanly manner.

"To hell with the literary allusions," Shvedov barked from the back of the jeep. "You'll love Raibek for one reason. The Zone is covered in fog. No matter how many times you come here, you hear myths and legends, tales of global conspiracies and ancient blood feuds, devout lectures on jihad from Chechen bandits." Raibek, he promised, was different. "He doesn't give a damn about Mr. Putin or Mr. General Troshev or the *Izvestia* newspaper. He cares only about his villages, where he is the tsar, God, and boss of the land. Whatever it is—gas, food, protection—he'll find it for his people. No one pays taxes. They pay honor to their lord. Raibek is a classic Chechen feudal baron."

Raibek sat out the first war. He sided with neither Basayev nor the Russians. For a time he even lived in Germany. "Trade," he said, when I asked what had brought him to a town along the Rhine. Yet given the elaborate allegiances of the *teips*, Chechnya's ancestral clans, it was inevitable that he would be drawn into the war.[42] In August 1995 a Chechen warlord from Argun, Allauddin Khamzatov, staked a claim to the ridge along Upper Vedeno. Raibek was in Europe, but his father, the ninety-year-old patriarch of the *teip*, was home. He refused to give in to the interloper.

The result was painful to remember. Khamzatov shot Raibek's father dead, right in front of his family. The feud open, Raibek came home and, as is required by *adat*, evened the bloodletting. He and his men hunted down the warlord and killed him and his accomplices. His troubles with Basayev and Khattab, however, had yet to begin. The next spring, in March 1996, as Raibek drove into Grozny, dozens of Basayev's men encircled him. A shootout ensued, and he barely escaped. Then, in June 1996, he was arrested on Basayev's orders and thrown into a jail run by the commander in the town of Dargo near the Dagestan border. He spent nearly eight months in jail before escaping one night in February 1997. He fled on foot through the frozen mountains to Dagestan and a month later was back in Vedeno.

As the UAZik pulled into his compound, a fortified lair of stone, brick, and wood, it was clear Raibek was not expecting guests. He extended his arm around my shoulder, in the half hug that Chechen men perform in salutation, but he did not smile. Raibek was not in a buoyant mood.

He had reason to be angry. In the first, critical months of Putin's War, he and his lieges stood their ground. While Troshev's troops moved south by shelling from afar and bombing without pause, even before the Russian paratroopers landed on their ridge, Raibek and his men took on Basayev and Khattab and several hundred of their fighters. In February 2000, he boasted with a grin, he and his men "liberated" Vedeno.

The Russians had rewarded him with the job of deputy military and administrative head of the region. It was not a sinecure to envy. Basayev and Khattab were eager to retake Vedeno, the town that now housed thousands of Chechen paramilitaries and several thousand more Russian soldiers, who manned Moscow's military headquarters in the district. The paramilitaries, moreover, would pledge allegiance to whoever paid a premium.

The job was sure to bring criticism, and in Vedeno, disfavor often took the form of assassination. Raibek, I'd heard, had already survived five attempts on his life. "Six," said one of his bodyguards. Raibek had lost count. On the sole road that switchbacked from his compound down into Vedeno, the gravelly road we had come on, Raibek's convoy now came across mines with increasing regularity. The woods were thick with enemies, he said. Basayev and Khattab, Raibek said, stood behind most of the attempts on his life, but not all.

The most recent attack had been the work of his new patrons, the Russians. One night a few months earlier a helicopter had roused Raibek and his family from their sleep. He got up in time to see a pair of APCs roll into his yard, as Russian soldiers, doing the bidding of their commander in Vedeno, shot their way into his house. They stole his furniture, rifles, bullets, and, most distressing of all, his Mercedes. Raibek did not feel betrayed. He knew better. "I never gave them my trust," he said. "I just wanted my property back." He succeeded in retrieving the Mercedes. He traced it to Khankala, the Russian base on the outskirts of Grozny, and, with help from up the Russian chain of command, repossessed the prized sedan.

Raibek's brother was a boxer who'd fought all over the world, even winning championships, it was said, in Europe. Looking at Raibek, I did not doubt it. At forty-two, he was not particularly tall or broad-shouldered, but when he moved, muscles rippled across his arms, shoulders, and neck. He wore a maroon shirt opened to the waist, sweatpants, and Adidas flip-flops. Gray stubble covered his sharp cheekbones, and a half grin revealed two chipped teeth. Issa made sure to tell me Raibek's blue eyes were a sign of his *teip*, the Gunoi, who, legend had it, owed their ancestry to mixed marriages of Chechens and Russians. The Gunoi were deemed less than pure Chechens.

Raibek took me on a tour. We walked through an open yard that had neat rows cut in its concrete floor where small flowers bloomed. Grassy hills, sloping down the steep mountainside, surrounded the main building. It was a two-story house made of hand-cut beams and square stones. The house, without a fourth wall on the courtyard side, was open to the mountain air. Raibek apologized that it lacked windows.

"A work in progress," I said.

"War," he said.

Scores of children ran underfoot. Women, teenagers and grandmothers, worked in every corner. As in every other home I had seen in Chechnya, they were the ones kneading, washing, stoking the stove. Playroom, kitchen, dining area, and garage were all one vast room without walls. A trio of children stood at a pool table, wielding cue sticks twice their height. Beyond the pool table, a Nissan Patrol and an old Lada were parked.

We lunched at a long table covered with hot flat bread, tomatoes and cucumbers, green onions and cloves of garlic. Three girls emerged from the smoke of the woodstove with bowls of mutton soup and plates of rice stacked with mutton. Over lunch Raibek told of a recent spectacle. It was night, he said, when the gorge grew "noisy." The sky lit up. A firefight ensued–from one side of the valley to the other. The Russians were firing from their base nearby on their own command post in Vedeno. Only later did he learn the reason: The soldiers hadn't been paid for weeks. They were hungry.

THROUGHOUT LUNCH a secret smile played on Raibek's lips. Over the three rounds of black tea that followed, I sensed him taking me in. By the time he offered to drive me out to his new checkpoint at the edge of his territory, I wondered if he'd finished doing the math, calculating the price an American journalist would bring. All the same, I agreed to see his checkpoint, "the only post in Chechnya," he boasted, "not manned by Russians." An elderly woman—"one of the wives," Issa informed me—delivered two AK-47s to the table. Raibek took them in his hands, strapped on a pistol, holstered a knife, buttoned his shirt, and led me to the Nissan Patrol.

Shvedov was not overjoyed that I had accepted the invitation. The checkpoint, he said, was on the far edge of Raibek's ridge. It bordered the preserve of Basayev and Khattab. "You go with Raibek," he said, "at your own risk."

I was slightly reassured when Mogamed, Raibek's mammoth bodyguard, jumped into the Patrol. "Raibek's best fighter" Issa called him. "And one he trusts," Shvedov added. Cradling a shiny automatic rifle between his knees, Mogamed sat to my left. Shvedov sat on my right, and Issa reluctantly up front. As Raibek set off on the road, his foot barely touching the accelerator, the bodyguard sat in silence, scanning the bushes beside the road. My calm deserted me, however, when I realized we were stopping to pick up another guard, a young fighter. He carried five grenades across his chest, two knives, one pistol on his belt, and a Kalashnikov in his hands. He crawled, without saying a word, into the rear of the Patrol.

We drove on, past scatterings of sheep and goats and a string of stone villages along the green ridge. "These are my people," Raibek said, but he meant "This is my land." Soon we stopped again, in the village of Marzoi Mokh (Sweet Earth), to add yet another body to our mission. We walked into the grassy yard of a low-slung wooden house where Raibek's best fighters, a family of four brothers, lived. The brothers, each the size of an ox, emerged and after an elaborate exchange of half hugs and salutations, one of them joined us, squeezing in next to me. I was now surrounded by three of Raibek's men, each heavily armed.

As we left Sweet Earth, Raibek did not drive more than ten miles an hour. He let each tire turn slowly over the rock. The road was torturous, at times so rutted it seemed impossible to traverse. Raibek tacked across it carefully, as if the massive Patrol were a dinghy on rough seas. For long stretches we saw no people. The woods ran thick and silence filled the car. The farther we drove from Raibek's last village, as the wheels spit out the rocks from underneath them, the more anxious I became. The farther on we drove, the more I found myself staring at the back of Raibek's head. His neck was tanned and creased, ringed by a gold chain. As the woods grew close, I thought of the bounty hunters who, like their forefathers who had done in Hadji Murad, were now angling for Raibek. For several miles, as he eased the Patrol along the gravel, the only sound in the car was Shvedov chewing his dentures.

As we drove on, Raibek pointed to a series of craters beside the road.

"From the last war," Shvedov said.

"From last week," Raibek said.

At last we reached the checkpoint. Five young Chechens in torn T-shirts and plastic slippers manned it. "My partisans." Raibek laughed. "If they do not stand here, this road is Khattab's highway into Vedeno, and from there he moves into Grozny." We joined a half dozen fighters more on the crest of the ridge. "Congratulations," Issa said. "You now stand where no journalist has been."

I tried to enjoy the view. The steep hills, cloaked in bush and woods, stretched before us. To the north, beyond the haze of the hot afternoon and the banners of smoke from the burning oil wells, we could see the plains of northeastern Chechnya.

One of the thin boys guarding the ridge tugged at my sleeve. "Don't stand here long," he said. "We do get fire." Three days before there'd been an attack. Snipers had shot two of his colleagues. To the east, said Raibek, waving to the mountains on our right, lay Dagestan. His ridge, he boasted, was now the first line of defense against the last of the insurgents. The lands that rose and fell from here to the border constituted the last refuge of his sworn enemies Basayev and Khattab.

We drove back along the narrow road, just as deliberately as on the way out. We were still far from the village of Sweet Earth when Raibek stopped the car, suddenly and without explanation. He pulled over beside a bright grove at the edge of a cluster of stone and corrugated metal houses. The small houses made up the village of Haji Otar. Issa got out of the Patrol, and soon everyone else, without a word, did as well. Raibek sat beside the road on a jagged boulder. He tugged at the tall grass in front of the rock. I sat nearby, on another stone. Together we watched as Issa crossed the road and walked up the hillside across from us. He had gone to pray. He knelt before a tiered shrine, each level a different hue, that filled the hillside.

It was the tomb, Raibek explained, of Heda, the mother of the holy man Kunta Hajji. Known to scholars of Sufism as al-Shaykh al-Hajj Kunta al-Michiki al-Iliskhani, Kunta Hajji brought an alternative to Chechnya to the

Naqshbandi path, the Qadiri order. Issa had long lectured me about the benevolent nature of Kunta's teachings. "Kunta was like a Tolstoy, a Gandhi, a Martin Luther King of the Caucasus," he had told me one night in Shali. "He offered Chechens a different road. He believed in nonviolent resistance. Where Shamil was militant, Kunta was contemplative."

As usual, Issa had folded legend into fact. Little, to be sure, is known of the holy man who introduced the Qadiri order to the Chechens. But in the middle of the first war, in 1994, one of the last surviving Chechen historians, Vakhid Akayev, scoured the archives in Grozny and wrote a life of Kunta Hajji.[43] Born in the Chechen village of Isti-Su, Kunta was eighteen when he embarked on his first pilgrimage to Mecca, or hajj, in 1848. (When he returned, he earned the surname Hajji as an honorific.) Initiated into the Qadiri order on his first hajj, Kunta brought the new movement with him when he returned to Chechnya.[44]

For the Chechens, Kunta opened a realm of purification. He urged withdrawal from the world, self-cleansing through prayer. A Muslim, he preached, must "clean his soul and interior from the dirt and everything that is forbidden and . . . from evil intentions and falsehoods."[45] In earthly matters, Kunta urged his believers to cease their resistance to the infidels of the north. He considered the struggle not only futile but a sin. He did not embrace Russian rule but sought to develop a pacifist resistance. Kunta Hajji, above all, offered a way out to a people whose only hope of deliverance had been found in war.

Kunta's teachings gained so many followers that in the late 1850s a religious divide rent Chechnya. Islam had always separated Russians from Chechens, but the advent of the Qadiri order alienated Chechen from Chechen. The emergence of two Sufi orders threatened to split a brotherhood bound by *adat*. Kunta Hajji had grown to rival Imam Shamil. And so in 1859, months before giving up to the Russians, Shamil sent Kunta off on a second hajj.

"The divide lasts to this day," Raibek said, as we sat at arm's length on opposite rocks across from the shrine to Kunta's mother. Issa was still across the road, praying. For Qadiris, Raibek explained, Heda's shrine was the most sacred in Chechnya. Kunta's own grave lies somewhere in Russia's northwestern corner. In the winter of 1864 the Russians arrested Kunta near Shali, and Alexander II ordered him brought to Russia to serve a life sentence "under police supervision."[46] Because Kunta died in 1867, poor, starving, and surrounded by Russians, in a village in the far-off province of Novgorod, Chechens came here, to Heda's tomb, to pray to him.

Many among the Qadiris had long since strayed and become just as militant as their Naqshbandi brothers. (Dudayev, for example, the man who led Chechnya's rebellion in the first war, was a Qadiri.) Yet among Imam Shamil's spiritual descendants, Kunta Hajji's teachings still stirred enmity. Basayev and Khattab's fighters had tried to destroy Heda's tomb. "To this day," Raibek said, "they're not happy that Kunta offered us a way out."

FOURTEEN

TOWARD THE END OF *Hadji Murad*, Tolstoy describes a raid that lays waste to a Chechen village, in much the same manner as the *zachistka* in Aldy. The Russian soldiers destroy houses, wreck roofs, bayonet (in the back) a young boy, and burn the villagers' fruit trees and gardens. The raid's grim aftermath, as written by Tolstoy, oddly echoed the testimony from Aldy that I had gathered in my notebooks: "The wailing of women sounded in every house and in the square where two more bodies were brought. The young children wailed with their mothers. The hungry animals howled, too, and there was nothing to give them. The older children played no games and watched their elders with frightened eyes."

In the tale, once the Russians leave, the elders gather to debate what to do. They face the same dilemma as those who survived the massacre in Aldy: How to respond? "Nobody spoke a word of hatred for the Russians. The emotion felt by every Chechen, old and young alike, was stronger than hatred. It was not hatred, it was a refusal to recognize these Russian dogs as men at all, and a feeling of such disgust, revulsion and bewilderment at the senseless cruelty of these creatures that the urge to destroy them—like the urge to destroy rats, venomous spiders or wolves—was an instinct as natural as that of self-preservation."[47] And so the blood feud widened. Tolstoy's villagers chose to follow Imam Shamil and his *Ghazavat.*

ON A PARCHED AFTERNOON in the steppe of Chechnya's northeastern corner, in the Cossack *stanitsa* of Starogladovskaya, I met Khusein Zagibov. Unlike Raibek, Khusein, a lean forty-eight-year-old former journalist, was overjoyed to have unannounced guests. Khusein ran the Tolstoy Museum in Starogladovskaya, sleeping in it at night with a shotgun by his side. He could not remember the last time he had been paid, but he had spent three winters fending off looters. Born during the exile in Central Asia, he had no illusions about the Russians' goodwill. Nor did he defend his compatriots. His brother had been kidnapped after the first war. The toll, Issa warned, was heavy. Khusein's eyes were rheumy with apprehension, and his long face bore a look of perpetual defeat. Yet he seemed to believe in the providence of the gods of literature. He took it as a sign of Tolstoy's saintliness that the museum honoring the writer's appreciation of the Chechen people still stood.

"I am writing in the stanitsa of Starogladovskaya, at ten in the evening on the thirtieth of June," Tolstoy wrote in his diary of 1851. "How did I end up here? Don't know. Why? Also, no idea."[48] Tolstoy came to Chechnya in the company of tsarist troops. He was twenty-four and, having run up unseemly gambling debts, felt an urgent need to leave Moscow. Here, in Starogladovskaya, in extended stretches from 1851 to 1853, Tolstoy first saw war. He also wrote his first book, *Childhood.* The young count, loosed from the strictures of Moscow, fell in love with the freedom and courage of Cossacks and Chechens alike.

Despite Khusein's stand, the museum languished in a desperate state. Gaping holes threatened to cave in its ceiling. The floor had rotted through. There was no electricity, let alone an alarm. Every night Khusein bedded down in the back office, lying beside a makeshift stove. The shotgun was handy, he said. It kept the thieves at bay. Yet there were no real artifacts of Tolstoy's to guard, only yellowing photocopies of pages he wrote here, a reproduction of a Cossack saddle, a white Cossack tunic. The prized object was a red carpet featuring Tolstoy's image as a young officer, beardless and dashing, as seen by a collective of Soviet seamstresses a century after his death. The carpet had been stolen in the first war, Khusein said. But a few weeks ago, after a *zachistka*, it had reappeared on a street nearby.

We made our way through the dark rooms with care. As Khusein spoke of the Great Writer, emotion filled his voice. "We are proud Tolstoy chose to live among us," he said, "and that he remembered his entire life the lessons our people taught him."

Tolstoy in his works on the Caucasus blamed neither Cossack nor Chechen. In his 1863 tale *The Cossacks*, he marveled at the Cossacks' fortitude on the empire's edge. Yet he depicted both Cossack and Chechen as just and their cultures as equally exotic and endangered. Tolstoy left little doubt: Moscow's heavy hand would bring only ruin to the peoples of the south. In a draft of *Hadji Murad*, he wrote:

. . . what always happens when a state, having large-scale military strength, enters into relations with primitive, small peoples, living their own independent life. Under the pretext of self-defense (even though attacks are always provoked by the powerful neighbor), or the pretext of civilizing the ways of a savage people (even though the savage people is living a life incomparably better and more peaceable than the "civilisers") . . . the servants of the military states commit all sorts of villainy against small peoples, while maintaining that one cannot deal with them otherwise. That was the situation in the Caucasus . . . when Russian military commanders, seeking to win distinction for themselves and appropriate the spoils of war, invaded peaceful lands, ravaged villages, killed hundreds of people, raped women, rustled thousands of cattle, and then blamed the tribesmen for their attacks on Russian possessions.[49]

Khusein was eager to draw out the visit, to keep life in these rooms as long as he could. But I had hoped to leave Chechnya that day, before the sun set and the curfew fell. As we came around to the threshold again, Khusein recited Tolstoy's memory of his days in Chechnya: "Never, neither before nor afterward, did I attain such heights of thought. . . . And everything I discovered then has remained my conviction."

As we stepped outside, the hot sun of the late afternoon enveloped us. Shvedov was happily smoking a *papirosa* beside the silver-painted statue of the Great Writer that dominated the museum yard. Tolstoy had offered a prophecy that still entranced Khusein. He had seen the futility of any military resolution to the discord in the south and foreseen the cost of imperial ambition. He had understood the Chechens' traditions and honored them. Chechnya loomed large in Tolstoy's imagination until his last days. When the writer, in his last escape from Yasnaya Polyana, his estate south of Moscow, died in 1910 in the snows at the train station at Astapovo, he was heading for the Caucasus. "At least there was one Russian," said Khusein, "who understood what it means to be Chechen." Emotion again filled his voice. This time it was not love but regret.

The Russians, he said, had reason to be unhappy with the pseudostate Maskhadov and Basayev and Khattab had won. "No order, no law, no *adat*, no *Shari'a*" had existed in his land after the first war. Russia had been right, Khusein said, to cut Chechnya off. No one but the Taliban had recognized the free state of Ichkeria. In the yard, someone had lined up a row of uprooted headstones, leaning against an old wooden fence. The stones were broken and engraved with Arabic script. Our commanders grew rich, he said, but who built a school or a hospital, let alone a museum? And now there was only *proizvol*, the arbitrary rule, of the generals and the warlords.

Shvedov had joined Issa and Yura in the UAZik. As I climbed back in the jeep, Khusein stood still, a hand at his forehead to shield against the sun. His museum may have lacked artifacts, but it was something singular and irreplaceable, a haven of humanity. As we pulled away, he remained in the yard, motionless beside the silvery statue of Tolstoy.

WE DROVE ACROSS the brown northern steppe. Hot air streamed through the open windows as the dry fields blurred left and right. The hay, uncut, had grown tall. The air seemed thin, filling the car with the smell of the fields. The road followed the Terek, and in the sky above it a hawk traced the turns of the narrow river. We had driven a half hour from the museum when a checkpoint appeared through the windshield. Suddenly a helicopter, only faintly heard moments earlier, swooped down across the road in front of us.

"Bastard," Issa mumbled. He was tired and ready, I was sure, to say good-bye.

The chopper flew wide to the right, before circling back and descending directly toward us. Yura drove steady on. The helicopter lifted its nose and rose suddenly, passing us by. As we neared the checkpoint, we pulled even with a battered Ural motorcycle. Its sidecar attached, the bike was overloaded with a Chechen family. A man drove it. Behind and beside him four children and an old woman clung tight. I looked at the woman–she had pulled her gray hair under a scarf and folded the hem of her long skirt under her legs—and wondered whose mother she was, the children's or the man at the wheel.

At the checkpoint the soldiers, three OMON officers from Lipetsk, wore black plastic sunglasses. They were in no mood for Issa's humor. They peered into the back of the UAZik. The officer on my side of the car, a blond fellow who revealed two gold lower teeth, asked for my documents. I complied.

"What the hell are you doing here?" he asked. His colleague had raised his Kalashnikov. It was now centered on Shvedov's chest.

"We've been to see Tolstoy," Issa said.

"Think you're funny, Grandpa?" the blond officer retorted.

Shvedov came to the rescue. "Look, fellas, look at this," he said as he undid a tiny pin from the pocket of his tattered army jacket. It had been a gift from Khusein, a button of soft gray metal that bore a relief of Lev Niko-layevich's profile. "From the museum," Shvedov said. "Keep it."

The OMON officers crowded close to examine the pin. They turned it over twice in their fleshy hands. They were intrigued.

"Tolstoy actually lived here?" the blond officer asked.

"What the hell for?" one of his colleagues said.

"I don't believe it," a third said.

I imagined Khusein taking in the scene. It was a shame, he'd said as we parted, no one seemed to read the Great Writer anymore.

FIFTEEN

We cannot term the Russian soldier, by any perversion of language, a brave and gallant warrior [wrote Edmund Spencer in 1836.] But then, on the other hand, he possesses many qualities highly valuable in the military subordinate: he is robust by nature; and, being accustomed to the hardest fare from infancy, bears patiently the severest privations; he is also bigot, slave, and fatalist; knows no will of his own. The first lesson that falls on his ear, is obedience to his lord, and love for his emperor; and, when led to the field, he becomes a complete machine, capable of being driven to the mouth of the cannon, or transformed into a target![50]

I SPENT MY FIRST NIGHT out of Chechnya in Mozdok, the Russian army town just across the border in North Ossetia that had long been the staging ground for the war. For twenty dollars I got a room in the center of town. Ever since the first war Rima and Viktor had turned their house into an informal bed-and-breakfast for journalists and relief workers. They seemed like good, gentle people, but there was no mistaking that I had left behind a different world.

Rima ordered me to take a shower, while she filled a large metal bowl with chopped cucumbers, tomatoes, and onions. Viktor was busy preparing for the evening's festivities. In the small courtyard, he dragged tall glass jars of home brew.

What was the party? I wondered after I'd showered for the first time in weeks. Her younger boy's eighteenth birthday, Rima said. His brother had already served in Chechnya. "He was sent there, and we didn't even know," she said. "He wouldn't tell us."

Viktor busied himself with an elaborate rubber contraption to fill a row of bottles with the moonshine.

"Now they'll come for my youngest," Rima said. "Who needed this?" she asked, staring at the broken linoleum of her kitchen floor.

Before I could say anything, Viktor, who had been born in Grozny and served his years in the Red Army in East Germany, answered for me. "No one," he said as he left the kitchen, "no one needed it."

CHECHNYA WOULD HAVE been sufficiently surreal, even without Sergei Tsygankov. Few Russian officers in Putin's War could claim a good job. But Tsygankov, a lieutenant colonel only months from retirement, may have had the worst one of all. Throughout the first winter of Putin's War, he ran the body collection point closest to the battleground. No matter whether the temperature fell below zero or rose over a hundred degrees, Tsygankov, with a supporting crew of twelve unfortunates, ran the tents that were the Mozdok base's approximation of an army morgue. It was his job to collect, sort, and send on north the dead to the Good Doctor's morgue in Rostov.

From the outside of the apartment block, nothing foretold the nightmares that resided inside. It was a long, drab block, home to officers, their wives and children. I knocked a second time before the door opened. A blond woman, in her early forties and wearing a yellow sundress, appeared. Both she and the unshaded lightbulb above her head were swaying.

"Sergei cannot be disturbed," she said.

I understood. He was drunk. And so, it seemed, was she. I told her I'd be back in the morning, early. The birthday party was still in embers the next morning when I peeled a thin sheet from my body, got dressed, and headed back across town. By seven Tsygankov stood in front of me. A tall, thin man, he opened the door in a sleeveless undershirt and khaki trousers.

"Five minutes," he said, shutting the door. A few minutes later he reappeared, in uniform. The morning was hot, near ninety degrees. We drove toward the Mozdok base, stopping a half mile from its gate. We sat down by the side of a swiftly moving creek. It was the Terek, the thin river that runs strongly through Vladikavkaz and across the breadth of Chechnya. We sat on the grassy bank for two hours, as the words poured from Tsygankov. Rarely did he stop for breath. Not once did he utter the words "corpse," "bodies," even "the dead."

Tsygankov was all limbs, like a stick figure. His eyes were a poor, dulled brown; his face was so attenuated there was no flesh to it. When he talked, you could see his bones at work. He had run the makeshift morgue for five months. His nerves were shot. In all, more than two thousand bodies had passed through his tent.

He told me what I knew: "They're lowering the figures." And what I did not know: "For every ten soldiers we get, only three have been killed in battle. All the rest have frozen to death, or died because someone wasn't careful with a weapon, or died from disease, especially in winter. Even from the flu." The dead, Tsygankov explained, fell into two categories: killed and deceased. "Killed" meant they had died in battle, but "deceased" meant they had died in the hospital. And if a wounded man died in the hospital, he was not included in the casualty figures.

Sometimes, Tsygankov said, the dead arrived in horrific form. Sometimes, for instance, when a poor soul had suffered a direct hit by a rocket-propelled grenade, they came in pieces. No flak jacket, he said dryly, could save you. The arms and legs would be blown right off. Sometimes the bodies revealed evidence of executions. One guy, he remembered, had come in with a notebook still stuffed in his breast pocket. A 5.45-caliber bullet had pierced its pages and then his heart.

"A Kalashnikov," he said, "at short range."

Drinking became Tsygankov's salvation. Everyone who worked the morgue drank, day and night. No one ever gave them a hard time about it. Morale was not low, he said. It did not exist.

"I'm gone, I know that," he said. "But what kind of life is it for the young guys? You never leave this work behind. You go home, take a shower, and then at night you're back in that tent again. You can shower, use vinegar, but it's no use. You can't get rid of the smell. And forget about saving money. Guys work two weeks straight. When they get two days off, of course they're going to go out, get drunk, and throw their whole paycheck away with a whore."

Tsygankov offered a grim measure of how far the Russian Army had fallen since Afghanistan. A career officer, he was a long way from his specialization. At eighteen he had graduated from the elite academy of the Soviet missile forces in 1971. After the academy he had served first in the north, near Arkhangelsk, then in Tajikistan, during the Soviet war in Afghanistan. He had been there when Gorbachev ordered the pullout, ending the Soviets' greatest military debacle. He had, as he put it, "absolutely nothing to do with this business."

His tour in the first Chechen war had erased any vestigial notions of patriotism or duty. Yet nothing had prepared him for the macabre service to come. The worst, he said, were the shortages. He told how he had to fuel his refrigerator truck by trading body bags for gasoline with other officers. The bags were in demand; the officers used them to insulate makeshift banyas at their encampments inside Chechnya. The bosses were forever promising gas money, he said. They even sent an officer in from Moscow to bring him cash. "Never saw the guy," he said. He took the money and never made it to Mozdok.

For most of the nearly one hundred thousand Russian troops in the region, Mozdok was merely the last transit point before Chechnya. For Tsygankov, it was home. His parents were from here, he had grown up here, and his grandfather had been the chief of police here. He had also married a local girl. Now they had a son and a daughter, two teenagers he could no longer afford to house, let alone educate.

Dark bags hung under his eyes. The left side of his face had developed a twitch. He laughed without cause, and more often than not, his answers did not follow my questions. He had seen more than enough in his waking hours, but now the nightmares terrorized him. At first the bodies, waxen and bloodied, had visited him only in his sleep. Then the daytime hallucinations began. He would be at work, in the hot tent, when suddenly the bodies began to come alive.

"They'd start to move," he said, "writhing in pain on the stretchers, reaching up toward my face if I got too close."

He had suffered two heart attacks in the tent. The last one landed him in the hospital. But after two weeks, he had been sent right back to work. At last one night he exploded, "like a bottle," as he put it, "hitting concrete." A Chechen had driven up to the front gates of the Mozdok base. In the back of his Lada was a corpse he had found by the road. It was the body of a Russian officer, a senior lieutenant.

"A normal Chechen," Tsygankov said. "It happens."

The general in charge of the base called in Tsygankov to deal with the body. Because it was a hot night and he had been working almost nonstop for a month, Tsygankov was not wearing his cap. The commander unleashed a verbal assault. "Where's your goddamned cap?" he screamed.

"Comrade General," Tsygankov replied, "why give me a hard time? What am I, some kind of fucking kid standing here? Some punk? You and I are the same goddamned age." The general said he would fire him. Tsygankov, overjoyed, urged him to go ahead. The paperwork went out, but the order came back, overturned.

"Who else they'd get to do that job?" Tsygankov said.

Before long he tried to take early retirement. His superiors would not let him. Unable to get fired or to quit, he was promoted—to the deputy commander, in charge of the rapid reaction force, of the base.

Tsygankov had been to a psychiatrist. "Sergei Vladimirovich," the psychiatrist had told him, "you must take a vacation, spend time in nature, go on picnics, go fishing."

Tsygankov laughed. His pension, he said, would be eighty-nine dollars a month. It was not enough to take care of his family, let alone to take a holiday. Now he wanted just enough money for "the only cure," to drink.

For all the ravages the war had brought him, Tsygankov still yearned for the old days, the days when he had entered the academy. "For a young kid," he said with a short laugh, "to be an officer was the height. It was real work for real men." The girls back then didn't love carpenters or welders. They loved soldiers. It wasn't just the uniform or the honor that attracted young brides. Military men earned more and retired younger. They also earned enviable pensions and long vacations on the Black Sea.

Yet what Tsygankov missed most was the professionalism. Mozdok, he said, was a *bardak*, a complete and utter mess, where SNAFUs, in their original U.S. Army sense, were the norm. A week earlier Anatoly Kvashnin, head of the Russian chiefs of staff, had come visiting. He had flown in from Moscow to tour the troops. The helicopter carrying him tried to land in Mozdok. It could not. A group of drunken *kontraktniki*, who had finished their tour of duty but been denied a flight home, refused to let Russia's top general land. "They got stuck here for days," Tsygankov said. "There were no planes. So what did they do? Got shit-faced. Then they heard the big boss was choppering in. So they got clever. They covered the landing pad with their bodies. He couldn't land." In the end, the *kontraktniki* got what they wanted, a plane out. "There was no other way," Tsygankov said. "It's a *bardak*, an absolute *bardak*."

FROM ROSTOV TO Vladikavkaz to Gudermes I had heard Russian officers offer their prognosis for "how the war would end." Tsygankov, too, had his theories. But sitting beside him in the thick grass along the Terek, I heard a rare sermon, a blend of propaganda, legend, and experience collected at ground zero. He may have ranted, but his prophecy was not easy to dismiss.

"Just look at history. Go back to the first Great Caucasian War, when Shamil was captured. Yermolov moved wisely back then. But this war is far from over. Even under the tsar, the conclusion was: You have to pack up all these tribes and disperse them across Russia. That's what Stalin eventually did.

"As long as the Chechens lived in Central Asia, there was no problem. As soon as they came back here, they went back to thievery, not least because they had been spoiled by the fat compensation the state gave them. They had grown lazy. Before then this land produced something. Cossacks, and even Chechens, worked it. Slowly the level of civilization rose. But now? The land is absolute shit. There's nothing left. The only idea still alive in Chechnya is the worst one for Russia, Wahhabism."

Tsygankov was facing a hard year. His son was moving to Petersburg, to enroll at the Suvorov military academy. Given Russia's culture of bribes, Tsygankov had gone deep into debt to pay nearly fifteen hundred dollars for a place there. His daughter had another year in high school. Then he'd have to bribe her way into the local institute as well. I asked if he would rather have his son close by. For a moment he thought it over.

"In Vladikavkaz there's another military academy," he said. "But I don't want him there. It's the Caucasus. And the Caucasus is still the Caucasus. It's eternal war."

SIXTEEN

AFTER A MONTH ON the road I did not leave the south with much hope. When I returned home to Moscow and Russian friends asked, "What will become of Chechnya?" I could find few encouraging words. But as Chechnya settled in my mind into a stream of dust, fighters, helicopter gunships, and tattooed OMON officers, I found myself thinking most often of Andrei Zhivoi.

His name alone astonished. *Zhivoi* means "alive." He was a former sapper who had lost his legs to a mine in Grozny in the first war. It took me the better part of a day trip from Rostov to find him in Taganrog, the town of Chekhov's birth off the Sea of Azov. He had come home from the war with a grievance but had not sunk into regret. He walked now with new legs, German prostheses procured by the Soldiers' Mothers Committee in Rostov.

I found him in Taganrog's one-room Center for Social Rehabilitation. The office was hidden behind a police station and above a row of garbage bins. It was filled with young people working silently. There were none of the computers and fax machines that decorated the offices of "grass-roots" initiatives favored by Western foundations across Russia. The center gave free legal advice to the disabled, the retired, and the indigent, anyone who walked through its door. Zhivoi had little time for me. He was preparing for court.

Before Chechnya, he had been certain to become a metal worker at the local factory. But he had come home from the war with a grievance. He had served not one but two tours, and the second extended, as was all too common, beyond the legal limit. His commander had simply refused to let him go home. Some may have called Zhivoi unlucky. As a deminer he'd been among the first into Grozny on successive waves. He did not see his fate as misfortune, nor did he blame the Chechens. He blamed the desperation of Russia's armed forces, their stubborn refusal to obey their own laws. If Russia had had a rule of law, Zhivoi was sure, he would still have had his legs.

He had recovered, learned to walk again, and gone to law school. He did not seek retribution or compensation but a weapon to rectify the ills he and so many others had suffered. The journey had not been easy. Taganrog, when Chekhov was born there in 1860, had been a sleepy hamlet of traders and fishermen. Then the city had been a disheveled corner of the south—"not a single sign without a spelling mistake," the playwright later recalled.[51] The Soviet century had little changed its provincial air. When Zhivoi returned home, no one knew his rights, and he had no one to turn to but the Mothers Committee in Rostov.

Born in a village outside Taganrog, he had moved to the city as a young boy for schooling. He'd grown up in his grandmother's home, a ramshackle collection of red brick that now housed an assortment of relatives. The yard reeked of rotting cabbage, the outhouse, and too many cats to count. It seemed an unlikely place to begin anew. The hardest he said was the first winter, when going to the toilet meant dragging himself across the frozen courtyard. For a time he'd returned to his parents' village. There he met his wife. A nursery school teacher, she had learned accounting to help pay the bills. He'd won a stipend for law school, but his military pension came in just under twenty dollars each month.

If the Chechen question is ever to be resolved, I imagined, it would take the strength of men like Zhivoi. He had lost nearly everything but returned to the living with dignity and hope. Zhivoi, at least, saw only one future—not just for Chechnya but for Russia as well. The country, he said, had to follow the rule of law. His insistent words on that stifling day in the south lingered as I traveled again across his country.

"Without that foundation," Zhivoi said, "without a legal order, it's impossible to achieve anything. Anything at all."

AFTERWORD

BY NOW WE HAVE a postmassacre routine. Be it in Africa, the Balkans, the Middle East, or Asia, the bloodletting is depicted in full color and its players are tidily divided into teams: killers and the killed. The body count is tallied, weighed against precedent, and then tucked away in the ever-expansive catalog of atrocity. As we struggle to explain such crimes, we reach for the convenient clichés of the failed new world order, while the victims and their murderers fade from view. We blame "global geopolitics," an "ancient ethnic hatred" or a "religious divide." Rarely do we pause long enough to seek the cause of the horror. With the exception of the Israeli-Palestinian conflict, which often takes center stage, rarely does our interest in massacres sustain us. It may turn from revulsion to curiosity, but rarely do we reach examination before acceptance, and resignation, settle in.

Aldy was no different. From Washington think tanks to Chechen kitchens, even the best informed reached for the catchphrases of the post–Soviet era to explain Aldy. To many, it was true that what had happened in the village on February 5, 2000, was "just another massacre." But this time even Russian officials recognized it was a war crime. Common Article 3 to the Geneva Conventions, the protocol governing internal armed conflicts, is eminently clear. Summary executions, even of armed combatants, even in war, are not acceptable practice. It was true, of course, civilians had been slaughtered in Chechnya before, and more would be afterward. Yet this time, at least in the first weeks that followed the massacre, the official response took a hopeful turn. Families of thirteen victims received death certificates stating that their relatives had been killed in a "mass murder." The yellow-white slips of paper read:

On February 5, 2000, the mass murder of civilians took place during a passport inspection by sub-units of the Ministry of Defense and the Ministry of the Interior of the Russian Federation in the village of Novye Aldy, Zavodskoi District, Grozny.

T. A. Murdalov
Investigator for Especially Important Matters,
Office of the North Caucasus Prosecutor General of the Russian Federation

A second unprecedented move followed. The military prosecutor of the North Caucasus dared blame Russian forces for the killing–specifically, OMON units from Petersburg and Ryazan. Yet because OMON units belong to the regional police forces, they do not come under the purview of the military prosecutor. So, even as he blamed the Russian police units, the military prosecutor washed his hands of Aldy. The case was transferred to the civilian prosecutor, who in turn shuffled it from Gudermes to Moscow to a backwater district in southern Russia and back again to Grozny, where, in 2002, it quietly came to rest.

NOTES

1. The Soviet armed forces were renowned for an abundance of generals. Dudayev, however, was the sole Chechen general, a major general since 1987. Born in the Chechen village of Permomaiskoye in 1944, as an infant he was sent into Central Asian exile with his family. He rose through the ranks of the air force to command, for a time in the last Soviet years, a squadron of Soviet nuclear bombers stationed in the town of Tartu in the Soviet republic of Estonia.

2. Ichkeria became the politically correct name for Chechnya, employed to mark a speaker's pro-independence stance.

3. Dumas traveled across the Caucasus just months before Imam Shamil, the famed leader of the mountioneers' nineteenth-century resistance, surrendered in 1859.

4. Detained by Russian soldiers on January 16, 2000, as he left the ruins of the Chechen capital, Grozny, Babitsky was held incommunicado for twelve days. He was jailed in a filtration prison in the village of Chernokozovo, where the Russians claimed to sort terrorists from civilians. Human rights groups reported widespread torture in the prison. On February 3, the day he was to be released, the Russians suddenly swapped Babitsky for two Russian POWs. The exchange, videotaped by the FSB, was later shown on Russian television. His colleagues, who saw Babitsky handed over to masked men in camouflage, purportedly the same Chechen fighters Moscow terms terrorists, were outraged. "What kind of state arrests a journalist and then uses him in a POW swap?" Radio Liberty's Moscow editor, Mikhail Sokolov, asked me. Later, few doubted that the FSB had faked the handover.

5. The ban on press travel was total. It extended even to Russian reporters. Any reporter who wished to travel to Chechnya was required to get a special Kremlin military accreditation and travel in the company of official Russian military escorts. The result: Much of the reporting, both foreign and Russian, came from reporters stationed in Khankala, the Russian military command headquarters outside Grozny. In Khankala the Russians conveniently maintained their own press center and the only television satellite relay dish in Chechnya. All those who violated the Kremlin's strict rules on access to the war zone—and many Western and Russian reporters did—did so at their own risk. Some, like Babitsky, suffered extreme consequences. Others, like my colleague Petra Procházková, were denied entry visas to Russia. In 2000, Procházková, a Czech journalist who during the first war had worked in Chechnya as much as any foreigner, decided to abandon journalism and move to Grozny to set up a food distribution center for the elderly and most vulnerable returnees. In 2001 the Russians denied her an entry visa to Russia for five years, although her husband was a Russian citizen, residing in Ingushetia. In the spring of 2002 the *Novaya gazeta* reporter Anna Politkovskaya, after investigating reports that

Russian officers in the Shatoi region had killed a number of civilians, received death threats and had to flee the region.

6. Like Elbrus, Mount Kazbek, after a century of isolation, was now enjoying the attention of the world's most enterprising climbers and skiers.

7. See Daniel Yergin, *The Prize: The Epic Quest for Oil, Money, and Power* (New York: Simon and Schuster, 1991), pp. 334–39.

8. Historians note the participation of the so-called Viking Division, a Nazi division that comprised a "volunteer" battalion of Finns and other Nordic and European volunteers. The question of how many Chechens, Ingush, and others from the North Caucasus aided the Nazis, at the center of Russian contentions about the Chechens' loyalty, has been explored at length in recent years. Western, Chechen, and even Russian historians, however, do not believe that substantial numbers of Chechens sided with the Nazis. See Dunlop, *Russia Confronts Chechnya: Roots of a Separatist Conflict* (Cambridge, U.K.: Cambridge University Press, 1998), pp. 58–61, who cites among others the Chechen historian Abdurahman Avtorkhanov.

Avtorkhanov writes: ". . . during the Second World War not one single German soldier ever appeared on Chechen-Ingush territory, with the exception of a brief occupation of the frontier locality of Malgobek, where the population was Russian" (Avtorkhanov, "The Chechens and the Ingush during the Soviet Period and Its Antecedents," in *The North Caucasus Barrier: The Russian Advance Towards the Muslim World*, ed. Marie Bennigsen Broxup [London: Hurst and Company, 1992], p. 147).

9. Dunlop, *Russia Confronts Chechnya*, pp. 61–67.

10. Robert Conquest, *The Nation Killers: The Soviet Deportation of Nationalities* (London: Macmillan & Co., 1970), p. 67.

11. In November 1989, the South Ossetian parliament voted to elevate the region's status to an "autonomous republic" within Georgia. The leader of Georgia at the time, the ultranationalist former philologist Zviad Gamsakhurdia, could not tolerate such insubordination among an ethnic minority. In days, Georgian troops marched on the South Ossetian capital, Tskhinvali. The ensuing conflict lasted, on and off, for three years, leaving thousands dead and forcing thousands more–both Ossetian and Georgian–from their homes. A cease-fire was struck in 1992, with Russian, Ossetian, and Georgian peacekeepers installed along the disputed region's borders. No peace deal, however, was signed, and as became the rule in the ensuing conflicts across the Caucasus, the crucial question of the region's status was left undetermined. South Ossetia meanwhile, cut off from Georgia, survived on little save a robust trade in bootleg vodka. The new Georgian president Eduard Shevardnadze, still beloved in Western capitals as Gorbachev's foreign minister, managed an uneasy peace with the first South Ossetian leader, Ludvig Chibirov. However, when· Eduard Kokoyev, a thirty-eight-year-old Moscow businessman and Russian citizen, was voted his successor in December 2001, tensions again heightened. Kokoyev, a former Komsomol leader who headed the largest contingent of South Ossetian fighters in the war, wasted little time in striking a new strident tone. In an interview published on March 6, 2002, in the Moscow newspaper *Vremya novostei*, he denounced Shevardnadze, saying he bore responsibility for genocide. "He ought to recognize the genocide of the Ossetians and personally apologize," Kokoyev said. The region, moreover, had gained new prominence. In 2002, as part of America's war on terror, a handful

of U.S. Special Forces arrived only some sixty miles away, in Georgia's Pankisi Gorge. Long a sanctuary for Chechen refugees, the Pankisi was now reputed to be–most vocally by Moscow–a haven for Chechen fighters and Al Qaeda operatives. Chechen fighters, specifically the band under the occasional control of the warlord Ruslan Gelayev, were seen in the gorge in late 2001, but just how many Chechen fighters were hiding out among them remained a matter of dispute. See Jean-Christophe Peuch "2001 in Review: Shevardnadze Loses Room to Maneuver," RFE, January 18, 2001; Alan Parastayev, Institute for War and Peace Reporting, Caucasus Reporting Service, "US Deployment in Georgia Angers South Ossetia," March 22, 2002.

12. In his excellent book on the Caucasus, Sebastian Smith writes of the importance, and irony, of Wasterzhi in North Ossetia. See *Allah's Mountains: Politics and War in the Russian Caucasus* (London: I. B. Tauris and Co., 1998), pp. 80–83.

13. For a wonderful explication of the founding and inner workings of Ingushetia's *ofshornaya zona*, see Chrystia Freeland, *Sale of the Century: The Inside Story of the Second Russian Revolution* (London: Little, Brown & Co., 2000), pp. 94–104.

14. In my travels elsewhere in the former Soviet states, particularly Uzbekistan and Tajikistan, I had encountered the Wahhabi movement before. Begun by Abdul Wahhab (1703–1792), Wahhabism intended to cleanse the Arab Bedouin from the influence of Sufism, wrote Ahmed Rashid in his *Taliban*. "The spread of Wahhabism became a major plank in Saudi foreign policy after the oil boom in the 1970s" (Ahmed Rashid, *Taliban: Militant Islam, Oil and Fundamentalism in Central Asia* [New Haven: Yale Note Bene, 2002], p. 85).

15. Susan Layton, *Russian Literature and Empire: Conquest of the Caucasus from Pushkin to Tolstoy* (New York: Cambridge University Press, 1994), p. 142.

16. Troshev's remarks made headlines in Russia. They were also broadcast on the Voice of America, December 2, 1999.

17. Michael Whittock, "Ermolov–Proconsul of the Caucasus." *Russian Review: An American Quarterly Devoted to Russia Past and Present*, v. 18, no. 1 (January 1959), p. 59; John F. Baddeley, *The Russian Conquest of the Caucasus* (London: Longmans, Green and Co., 1908), p. 93.

18. Whittock, "Ermolov," p. 59; Moshe Gammer, "Russian Strategies in the Conquest of Chechnia and Daghestan, 1825–1859," North Caucasus Barrier, ed. Bennigsen Broxup, pp. 45–61.

19. Baddeley, *Russian Conquest*, p. 97.

20. Gammer, *North Caucasus Barrier*, p. 47; Whittock, "Ermolov," p. 58.

21. Baddeley, *Russian Conquest*, pp. 106–7.

22. Layton, *Russian Literature and Empire*, p. 108.

23. The Chechen among the three men in the statue was Aslanbek Sheripov. Next to him was an Ingush, Ghapur Akhriyev. The third man, naturally, was Russian, Nikolai Gikalo. All three were ardent Bolsheviks. The trio was intended to symbolize the unity of the three major ethnic groups of the Soviet province of Checheno-Ingushetia.

24. Maskhadov, like Dudayev, the political leader of the Chechens' rebellion, was a former Soviet officer–in his case, a former artillery officer.

25. "We are absolutely independent," a Basayev envoy told me in mock seriousness after the first war ended, "because absolutely no one depends on us." General Lebed was well aware that his deal was faulty. But he claimed that the Kremlin had hindered his negotiating leverage. "We could only wait and let the smoke clear," Lebed later told me. "Yeltsin would not allow me to do anything more."

26. The ties between Khattab and bin Laden have yet to be clearly established. Khattab, however, in an interview with the Chechen rebels' main Web site, Kavkaz.org, less than a month after September 11, 2001, was quoted as saying that bin Laden was "a good mujahid and scholar" and a "very decent" man, whom he had known when both fought the Soviets in Afghanistan, but that Khattab had not seen nor spoken with bin Laden for eight years (Kavkaz.org, October 10, 2001; see also *Jamestown Monitor*, v. 7, issue 187, October 11, 2001).

27. The fighters reportedly moved into the Dagestani regions of Botlikh and Buinak, taking over the villages of Karamakhi, Chabanmakhi, and Kadar. When serving as Yeltsin's interior minister, Sergei Stepashin had met with the Wahhabi leaders of Karamakhi and Chabanmakhi on August 20, 1998. For prescient reporting, see Mikhail Roshchin, "Wahhabism in Dagestan and Chechnya," Keston News Service, March 2, 1999.

28. The portfolio of the Kremlin Property Department ranged from the sprawling dacha complexes outside Moscow to luxury hotels to the presidential airlines. By his own hyperbolic estimation, Borodin oversaw property worth a total of $600 billion dollars. The so-called Mabetex scandal was an immensely complex affair but centered on allegations of money laundering and corruption at the highest level of the Yeltsin Kremlin. Borodin was detained in January 2001 at New York's JFK Airport on a Swiss warrant. The Swiss had accused him of involvement in a multimillion-dollar kickback and money-laundering scheme arising from Russian state construction jobs. Swiss authorities had alleged in court documents that Borodin had used "his position to obtain approximately $30 million in kickbacks from Swiss companies to which he awarded contracts." Prosecutors also claimed that Borodin had "attempted to conceal these kickbacks through a series of transfers along bank accounts belonging to offshore companies controlled by him and certain members of his family" (AP, April 2, 2001).

After three months, in April 2001, Borodin abandoned his extradition fight. In Geneva, he was released on bail. In March 2002, Geneva Cantonal Prosecutor Bernard Bartossa found Borodin guilty of laundering $22.4 million through Swiss banks while he ran the Kremlin property empire under Yeltsin. Bartossa fined Borodin 300,000 Swiss franks ($175,000) and closed the case (AP, March 15, 2002; RFE Newsline, March 7, 2002).

29. The Bank of New York affair, another of the great scandals of the late Yeltsin years, exploded on the front page of the *New York Times* on August 19, 1999 (see Raymond Bonner and Timothy L. O'Brien, "Activity at Bank Raises Suspicion of Russian Mob Tie"). The *Times* ran a series of extensive investigative articles, as the rest of the Western media joined the chase. The BoNY scandal dragged on for months, yielding voluminous articles in the press, but few indictments, let alone convictions. A former bank executive, Lucy Edwards, and her husband, Peter Berlin, both Russian émigrés, did plead guilty to money laundering, saying they were paid $1.8 million in commissions (Reuters, February 16, 2000). In the end, however, the scandal proved an unduly inflated story.

30. In a rare occurrence, the bombing in Buinaksk resulted in a trial. In March 2000, a

court in Makhachkala sentenced two men to life in prison for their roles in the blast. On November 14, 2001, the trial of five Karachaevo-Cherkessia residents accused of preparing terrorist acts ended. Three were sentenced to fifteen years, one to thirteen and one-half years, and another to nine years in prison. The court held that the men had graduated from a Wahhabi terrorist training camp run by Khattab in Avtury, Chechnya. The trial, however, failed to link the men to the apartment house bombings in Moscow and Volgodonsk. By 2004, although the federal prosecutor's office had completed their investigation of the 1999 bombings, and claimed to have apprehended at least two suspects, the crimes' initiators remain unknown.

31. After Patrushev's remarkable statement on September 24, 1999, a number of Duma deputies moved to open an inquiry into the Ryazan case. But in March 2000 the move failed, blocked by the pro-Putin Unity party. In the spring of 2002, Boris Berezovsky, by then a fallen oligarch out of favor with the Kremlin and in opposition to Putin, the man he had helped make president, financed an elaborate public relations campaign that sought to blame the FSB for the bombings in Moscow, Volgodonsk, and Buinaksk. On March 5, 2002, Berezovsky told a London press conference that the FSB had masterminded the bombings to justify the second war in Chechnya. Other than generate publicity for himself, Berezovsky's campaign added little depth to the hunt for the culprits behind the bombings.

32. In 2002, after the arrival of American military advisers there, the Pankisi Gorge gained some notice in the U.S. media. The gorge lies inside the former Soviet republic of Georgia, in the valley formed by the Alazani River in Georgia's northeastern province of Kakheti. Long before the Russian offensive in Chechnya, ethnic Chechens–known as Kisty in Georgian–had made the gorge their home. The Kisty first began to settle the small mountain villages, often no more than a handful of stone houses and a few flocks of sheep, more than a hundred years ago. During the second Chechen war, military officials in Moscow talked of hundreds, even thousands of Chechen and Taliban fighters who had taken refuge in the gorge to heal their wounds, train recruits, and smuggle arms, supplies, and money into Chechnya. Rumors continue to emanate from the gorge, but one fact is undisputed: During the second war, the Pankisi became a critical lifeline for the Chechens to the outside world. The Chechens came by the myriad of trails through the mountains, but also by car. They traveled along the newly paved road, one of Shamil Basayev's construction projects, that linked the Chechen mountain village of Itum-Kale with Shatili on the Georgian side. When I visited the village of Duisi at the mouth of the Pankisi in October 1999, the war had forced a first wave of as many as two thousand refugees. UN relief workers in the Georgian capital, Tbilisi, provided them with supplies and plastic sheeting. The Georgian government preferred to ignore their presence. In October 1999, the main road from Tbilisi to the Pankisi Gorge was nearly unmanned by Georgian police.

33. Moscow's previous puppet regime was headed by Doku Zavgayev, the republic's Communist Party chief from 1989 to 1991. Zavgayev's attempt at administration lasted from October 1995 to August 1996, when the rebels retook Grozny. For more on Zavgayev's abortive regime and Koshman's role in the "nonrestoration of Grozny," see Carlotta Gall and Thomas de Waal, *Chechnya: A Small Victorious War* (London: Frank Cass, 1997), pp. 314–15.

34. Present-day Chernorechiye and Novy Aldy, both districts of Grozny, encompass the territory of the original Aldy. Residents on both sides of the dam are descendants of

those who lived in the eighteenth-century village of Aldy. Novy Aldy was founded only in the 1950s, when the Chechens were allowed to return from their Central Asian exile.

35. Anna Zelkina, *In Quest for God and Freedom: Sufi Responses to the Russian Advance in the North Caucasus* (London: C. Hurst & Co., 2000), pp. 59–60.

36. Ibid., p. 64; See also: Dunlop, *Russia Confronts Chechnya,* pp. 11–12.

37. Zelkina, *In Quest for God and Freedom,* p. 66.

38. In April 1996, Khattab organized and led the ambush that trapped and destroyed a large Russian armored convoy near the village of Yaryshmardy. Nearly one hundred Russian soldiers were killed. Khattab, in a self-congratulary video, marched with a beaming smile beside a long line of Russian corpses. The video, quite likely made for fund-raising purposes in the Middle East, was broadcast often on Russian television. After September 11, 2001, the charges that bin Laden and the Chechen rebels were in league grew by the day. The reports, vigorously promulgated by Moscow but amply seconded by Washington, ran from the probable–that Al Qaeda financed and recruited men for Khattab–to the fantastic: that bin Laden had offered unknown Chechen agents "\$30 million and two tons of opium" for twenty Russian nuclear warheads (*Christian Science Monitor,* October 30, 2001). A series of reports, beginning with a UPI article in August 2000, held that a man known as Abu Daud, reportedly a bin Laden associate, had claimed to have trained four hundred fighters at an Al Qaeda camp in Afghanistan and sent them to Chechnya. While Abu Daud's claims went unproved, a number of Islamic militant groups had long been interested in Chechnya both as a cause and a potential center of operations. English-language Web sites, such as Qoqaz.net, openly conducted fund raising for the Chechen insurgency. It is also known, moreover, thanks to an Al Qaeda computer acquired in Kabul after the fall of the Taliban by my colleague in the Moscow press corps Alan Cullison, of the *Wall Street Journal,* that in December 1996 bin Laden's chief deputy, Dr. Ayman al-Zawahiri, tried to enter Dagestan. A letter Zawahiri sent to his colleagues in Egyptian Islamic Jihad, the militant group he helped found in Cairo years before allying with bin Laden, reveals that he had tried to resettle the group in Chechnya. In Dagestan, however, Zawahiri and two assistants were arrested for entering the Russian Federation without visas. He spent six months in jail in Makhachkala, the Dagestani capital, before being released. At the trial in April 1997, Zawahiri stated his aim in coming to Dagestan was "to find out the price for leather, medicine, and other goods." Only after his failed Dagestani escapade did Zawahiri turn to Afghanistan as a base of operations, and eventually establish a formal alliance with bin Laden, in early 1998. Egyptian Islamic Jihad and Al Qaeda officially merged into Qaeda al-Jihad in June 2001. The *Wall Street Journal,* on July 2, 2002, published the first detailed account of Zawahiri's failed mission, "How a Secret, Failed Trip to Chechnya Turned Key Plotter's Focus to America and bin Laden," written by Alan Cullison and Andrew Higgins. See also Lawrence Wright's piece on Zawahiri, "The Man behind Bin Laden," *New Yorker* (September 16, 2002.)

39. The administrator was Ruslan Khamidov, killed in Alkhan-Yurt on July 16, 2000. Such reprisals for siding with the Russians became widespread. In February 2000 in Grozny the Russians established an OMON unit made up of three hundred Chechens aligned with Moscow. By the end of 2002, however, sixty of the Chechen OMON officers had been killed by rebels in ambushes and assassinations. The youngest victim was Katya Batayeva, the eighteen-year-old secretary of the Chechen OMON commander. Batayeva died from sixteen bullet wounds in January 2001.

40. The filtration camps have been amply documented. Babitsky was the most vocal witness of the Chernokozovo prison, but Memorial, Human Rights Watch, and Amnesty International all have published numerous reports on the human rights abuses visited on the Chechens in these jails. See, for example, Amnesty's March 23, 2000, report, "Chechnya: Rape and Torture of Children in Chernokozovo 'Filtration Camp.' "

41. The film, *War in Chechnya: A Strange War,* was produced by the pro-Russian Information Center of the Chechen Republic in 1997.

42. Chechen *teips* are clans, but the word denotes more than familial history. A *teip* signifies one's ancestral land. Gall and de Waal, *Chechnya,* p. 26. The Russian scholar Jan Chesnov has written extensively on the history and significance of the *teips.*

43. *Sheikh Kunta Khadzhi: zhizn' i uchenie.* Against great odds, it was published in Grozny in 1994.

44. Ibid., pp. 28–31; Zelkina, *In Quest of God and Freedom,* pp. 229–30.

45. Anna Zelkina, "Some Aspects of the Teaching of Kunta Hâjjî: On the Basics of the Manuscript by Abdal-Salâm Written in 1862 AD," *Journal of the History of Sufism* (2000), p. 491.

46. Akayev, *Kunta,* p. 61.

47. Leo Tolstoy, *Master and Man and Other Stories,* tr. Paul Foote (London: Penguin Group, 1977), p. 226.

48. Lev Tolstoi, *Dnevniki (1847–1894), Sobranie sochinenii v dvadtsati dvukh tomakh* (Moskva: Khudozhestvennaia literatura, 1985), v. 21, p. 37.

49. Layton, *Russian Literature and Empire,* pp. 284–85.

50. Edmund Spencer, *Travels in Circassia, Krim-Tartary, & C.* (London: Henry Colburn, 1839), v. 2, p. 20.

51. Alexander Chudakov, "Dr. Chekhov: A Biographical Essay (29 January 1980–15 July 1904)," in *The Cambridge Companion to Chekhov* (Cambridge, U.K.: Cambridge University Press, 2000), p. 3.

TIMELINE

Seventeenth–Nineteenth century: Chechens adopt Sunni Islam, but retain many ancestral customs.

1784: Russia establishes a principal garrison in the North Caucasus. It is named *Vladikavkaz*, which means "to rule the Caucasus."

1785: Catherine the Great's forces encounter a new resistance movement among the mountaineers led by Chechen Sheikh Mansour. Major-General Pavel Potemkin suffers a bloody defeat at a village along the River Sunzha, site of the modern-day village of Aldy.

1818: Grozny is founded as a Russian fort.

1859: Following decades of armed struggle, Russia at last subdues the mountain fighters of Chechnya. Legendary fighter Imam Shamil surrenders to the Russians.

1919: Chechnya, Dagestan, and other adjacent nations declare the independent North Caucasus Republic.

1922: Soviet authorities establish an "autonomous region" for the Chechens, which in 1934 will be merged with their neighboring brethren, the Ingush, in the Chechen-Ingush Autonomous Soviet Socialist Republic.

1944: Red Army Day, February 23. Stalin deports the entire Chechen and Ingush populations to Central Asia and Siberia. The formal excuse: alleged collaboration with Nazi invaders. Thousands die in the process.

1957: Nikita Khrushchev restores the Chechen-Ingush Autonomous Soviet Socialist Republic. Chechens are permitted to repatriate to their homeland.

1989: Last Soviet census shows 1,084,000 people living in the territory of

Chechnya, of whom 715,000 were Chechens, 269,000 were ethnic Russians, and the rest Soviet citizens of other ethnic extraction.

1991: As the USSR collapses, in Chechnya Moscow loyalist and Communist leader Doku Zavgayev is overthrown.

1991: October 27. Djokhar Dudayev, the first Soviet Chechen general, wins a presidential poll and proclaims Chechnya independent. Moscow condemns the election.

1991: November. Three Chechen separatists hijack a Russian airliner and force it to fly to Turkey. The hijackers are permitted to return to Chechnya; one is Shamil Basayev, the future field commander.

1992: All regions in Russia formerly designated "autonomous republics" in the USSR sign a federation treaty, except Chechnya and Tatarstan. A new Chechen constitution is adopted; the independent, secular state is to be governed by a president and parliament.

1994: August–November. Supported by Moscow, pro-Russian Chechen irregulars stage unsuccessful efforts to end Dudayev's rule.

1994: November 27. Yeltsin and the Russian security council sign a secret decree pledging to restore "constitutional order" in the breakaway republic.

1994: December 11. Yeltsin sends forty thousand Russian troops into Chechnya.

1994: December 31. Russian armored columns launch an assault on Grozny. The first Chechen war commences. In twenty months of fighting, as many as one hundred thousand people–most of them civilians, including ethnic Russian residents of Chechnya–are estimated to have been killed.

1995: April. The Chechen village of Samashki is attacked by Russian Interior Ministry troops. Human rights organizations estimate 150 civilians are killed.

1995: June. Chechen rebels under the command of Shamil Basayev take more than a thousand Russian civilians hostage at a hospital in Budennovsk, a town in southern Russia. More than a hundred are killed in two botched rescue attempts by Russian special forces. Prime Minister Viktor Chernomyrdin publicly negotiates with Basayev, who along with the rest of the hostage takers is permitted to retreat to Chechnya. Basayev becomes Russia's most wanted man.

1996:   January. Chechen rebels stage a raid on the town of Kizlyar, Dagestan, and take nearly two thousand hostages. They are forced to retreat to Chechnya, after numerous hostages are killed.

1996:   April 21. Russian military intelligence assassinates Dudayev in a missile attack. Zelimkhan Yandarbiyev, an erstwhile writer and poet serving as Dudayev's vice president, succeeds him.

1996:   August 6. Chechen fighters stage a mass attack and retake Grozny. In the days that follow, the head of Yeltsin's security council, General Alexander Lebed, and the Chechen field commander Aslan Maskhadov sign a cease-fire. The pact is the cornerstone of what becomes known as the Khasavyurt Accords. The question of sovereignty, however, is postponed to 2001. Russian forces withdraw.

1996:   December. Six Red Cross foreign staff–five female nurses, one male architect–are murdered in their hospital headquarters in the village of Novye Atagi, eleven miles southwest of Grozny.

1997:   January. Presidential elections are held in Chechnya, monitored by the Organization for Security and Cooperation in Europe (OSCE). Maskhadov, a political moderate, wins. Basayev gains just 23.5 percent of the vote. Moscow recognizes the Maskhadov government.

1997:   May. In the Kremlin, Yeltsin and Maskhadov sign a peace treaty, but the question of the republic's ultimate status remains unresolved.

1998:   May. Valentin Vlasov, Yeltsin's chief envoy in Chechnya, is kidnapped and held for six months. In December, four engineers from Britain and New Zealand are kidnapped and beheaded. Kidnappings of aid workers, journalists, and Chechen civilians continue unabated.

1999:   March. In a brazen and well-planned operation, the Kremlin's new envoy in Chechnya, General Gennadi Shpigun, is kidnapped from the Grozny airport. General Shpigun's corpse is discovered in the spring of 2000 in the Shatoi region in the south of Chechnya.

1999:   January. Maskhadov, under pressure from more radicalized former field commanders, announces that *Shari'a* law will be introduced in the republic.

1999:   July. Chechen rebels cross into Dagestan but are repelled. The stated goal: Imam Shamil's dream of a pan-Caucasian Islamic republic.

1999:   September. In a series of apartment building blasts across Russia, nearly three hundred are killed in their sleep. First bombed is a building in Buinakst, Dagestan, housing Russian military and their families. Then in Moscow, and the southern city of Volgodonsk, three other apartment buildings are bombed. Russian law enforcement blames the Chechen rebels. Moscow again sends troops into Chechnya. The new Russian prime minister, Vladimir Putin, terms the deployment an "antiterrorism" operation, not a war.

1999:   October. Moscow refuses to negotiate with Maskhadov. As Russian forces flood into Chechnya, tens of thousands of Chechen civilians flee. As many as three hundred thousand become refugees in neighboring provinces.

1999:   December 31. Yeltsin resigns. Putin becomes acting president of the Russian Federation.

2000:   Late January–early February. With little resistance, Russian troops take Grozny. Chechen fighters retreat from the capital; many repair to the mountains in the south of the republic.

2000:   February 5. A *zachistka*–"mop-up operation,"–takes place in the village of Aldy, on the outskirts of Grozny. At least sixty Chechen civilians are killed.

2000:   May. Putin announces direct presidential rule from Moscow.

2000:   June 7. Khava Barayeva, a relative of two Chechen field commanders, detonates a truck bomb at a military checkpoint in Alkhan-Yurt. Barayeva becomes the first known Chechen female suicide bomber. The rebels claim twenty-seven Russian soldiers died; Moscow says only two are killed.

2000:   June 12. Former Chechen grand mufti Akhmed Kadirov, who fought on the rebel side in the first war, is named to head the pro-Moscow administration in Chechnya.

2002: April. The Saudi-born rebel commander known as Khattab is killed, reportedly poisoned in an assassination orchestrated by Russia's Federal Security Service (FSB).

2002: May. At a Victory Day parade in Dagestan, a bomb blast kills at least thirty-five people, including twelve children.

2002: August. A Russian Mi-26, one of the army's largest helicopters, is downed by Chechen fighters with a Russian-made shoulder-fired missile. More than a hundred Russian soldiers die.

2002: October. Forty-one terrorists, including eighteen women and led by twenty-five-year-old Movsar Barayev, seize a Moscow theater, holding nearly eight hundred people hostage for three days. All the terrorists and 130 hostages are killed when Russian forces use a gas to disable the terrorists and then storm the building.

2003: March. Referendum in Chechnya calls for a new constitution reaffirming the republic's inclusion within the Russian Federation.

2003: July. Two Chechen female suicide bombers kill themselves and fourteen others at an outdoor Moscow music festival.

2003: October. In an election condemned by Western human rights groups, Kadirov is elected Chechnya's new president.

2004: February. Former Chechen president Yandarbiyev is assassinated in Qatar. A Qatari court sentences two Russian intelligence agents to life for the crime. In a suicide bombing attack in the Moscow metro, a Chechen woman kills herself and more than forty subway riders.

2004: May 9. At a Victory Day parade in Grozny, President Kadirov is killed by a bomb explosion.

2004. June: Chechen fighters stage a mass raid in Nazran, the capital of neighboring Ingushetia. Russian authorities report at least forty-seven law enforcement officers and Ingush officials are among the dead.

TIMELINE

2004:   August 24. Two Russian airliners are brought down by explosions, killing all ninety people aboard. Russian authorities declare two Chechen women the bombers.

2004:   August 29. In a new presidential poll staged by Moscow, Kremlin favorite and former Chechen interior minister Alu Alkhanov is elected to succeed Kadirov.

2004:   August 31. A Chechen woman detonates a belt laden with explosives near a metro station in central Moscow, killing herself and at least ten others.

2004:   September 1. On the first day of the school year, a heavily armed band of terrorists—among them Chechens, Ingush, and reportedly at least one ethnic Slav—take nearly twelve hundred civilians hostage in a middle school in Beslan, North Ossetia. By the siege's end, an estimated one thousand civilians are killed or wounded—hundreds of them children. Putin blames the "intervention of international terrorists"; Maskhadov, who has continued to evade capture, condemns the school seizure but says it was carried out by "madmen" driven by a hunger for revenge.

Sources: BBC, *Chechnya Weekly* of the Jamestown Foundation, Institute for War and Peace Reporting, *New York Times*, Radio Free Europe/Radio Liberty, Radio Echo Moskvy, *Washington Post*.

FOR FURTHER READING

NB: *Where possible, I have listed English translations of works originally published in Russian, German, or French.*

Abubakarov, Taimaz. *Rezhim Dzokhara Dudaeva: pravda i vymesel,* Moscow: INSAN, 1998.

Akaev, V. *Sheikh Kunta-Khadzhi: zhizn' i uchenie.* Groznyi: Ichkeriia, 1994.

——. *Sufizm i vakhkhabizm na Severnom Kavkaze.* Moskva: Institut etnologii i antropologii im. Miklukho-Maklaia RAN, 1999.

Anderson, Scott. *The Man Who Tried to Save the World: The Dangerous Life and Mysterious Disappearance of Fred Cuny.* New York: Anchor Books, 1999.

Ascherson, Neal. *Black Sea.* New York: Hill and Wang, 1995.

Avtorkhanov, Abdurahman. "The Chechens and the Ingush during the Soviet Period and Its Antecedents." In *The North Caucasus Barrier: The Russian Advance towards the Muslim World,* ed. Marie Bennigsen Broxup. London: Hurst and Company, 1992.

Baddeley, John F. *The Rugged Flanks of the Caucasus.* London: Oxford University Press, 1940.

——. *The Russian Conquest of the Caucasus.* London: Longmans, Green and Company, 1908.

Bagalova, Zuleikhan, et al. *Chechnia: prava na kul'ture.* Moscow: Polinform-Talburi Publishers, 1999.

Barrett, Thomas M. "Lines of Uncertainty: The Frontiers of the North Caucasus." *Slavic Review,* v. 54, no. 3 (Fall 1995).

Bennett, Vanora. *Crying Wolf: The Return of War to Chechnya.* London: Picador, 1998.

Bennigsen, Alexandre. *Narodnoe dvizhenie na Kavkaze v XVIII v. : "Sviashchennaia voina" Sheikha Mansura.* Makhachkala: Fond "Tarikh," 1994.

——, and S. Enders Wimbush. *Mystics and Commissars: Sufism in the Soviet Union.* London: C. Hurst & Company, 1985.

Bey, Essad-. *Twelve Secrets of the Caucasus,* tr. G. Chychele Waterson. New York: Viking Press, 1931.

Blanch, Lesley. *The Sabres of Paradise.* New York: Carroll and Graf Publishers, 1960.

Blinushov, A., A. Guryanov, O. Orlov, Ya. Rachonsky, and A. Sokolov. *By All Available*

Means: The Russian Federation Ministry of Internal Affairs Operation in the Village of Samashki: April 7-8, 1995, tr. R. Denber. Moscow: Memorial Human Rights Center, 1996.

Burrell, George A. *An American Engineer Looks at Russia.* Boston: Stratford Company Publishers, 1932.

Cherkasov, Aleksandr, et al. *"Zachistka": Poselok Novye Aldi.* Moscow: Memorial Society, February 5, 2000.

Chudakov, Alexander. "Dr. Chekhov: A Biographical Essay (29 January 1860–15 July 1904). In *The Cambridge Companion to Chekhov.* Cambridge, U.K.: Cambridge University Press, 2000.

Conquest, Robert. *The Nation Killers: The Soviet Deportation of Nationalities.* London: Macmillan and Co., 1970.

Derluguian, Georgi. "Che Guevaras in Turbans: Chechens versus Globalization." *New Left Review,* no. 237 (September–October 1999).

Ditson, George Leighton. *Circassia: or, a Tour to the Caucasus.* London: T. C. Newby. New York: Stringer & Townsend, 1850.

Dudaev, Dzhokhar. *Ternisty put' k svobode.* Vilnius: Vaga, 1993.

Dumas (*pére*), Alexandre. *Adventures in the Caucasus,* ed. and tr. A. E. Murch. London: Peter Owen Limited, 1962.

Dunlop, John B. *Russia Confronts Chechnya: Roots of a Separatist Conflict.* Cambridge, U.K.: Cambridge University Press 1998.

Evangelista, Matthew. *The Chechen Wars: Will Russia Go the Way of the Soviet Union?* Washington, D.C.: Brookings Institution Press, 2003.

Furman, Dmitrii, et al., *Chechnia i Rossiia: obshchestva i gosudarstva.* Moskva: Polinform-Talburi, 1999.

Gall, Carlotta, and Thomas de Waal. *Chechnya: A Small Victorious War.* London: Pan Books, 1997.

Gammer, Moshe. "The Introduction of the Khalidiyya and of the Qâdiriyya into Daghestan in the Nineteenth Century." In *Daghestan and the World of Islam,* eds. Moshe Gammer and David J. Wasserstein. Helsinki: Finnish Academy of Sciences and Humanities (forthcoming).

——. *Muslim Resistance to the Tsar: Shamil and the Conquest of Chechnia and Daghestan.* London: Frank Cass, 1994.

——. "The Qâdiriyya in the Northern Caucasus." *Journal of the History of Sufism,* no. 1 (2000).

Goltz, Thomas. *Chechnya Diary: A War Correspondent's Story of Surviving the War in Chechnya.* New York: Thomas Dunne Books, 2003.

Graham, Stephen. *A Vagabond in the Caucasus, with Some Notes of His Experiences among the Russians.* London: John Lane, Bodley Head, 1911.

Greene, Stanley. *Open Wound: Chechnya 1994 to 2003.* London: Trolley Books, 2003.

Hartmann, R., R. Virchow, and A. Voss, eds. *Zeitschrift für Ethnologie: Organ der Berliner Gesellschaft für Anthropologie, Ethnologie und Urgeschichte.* Berlin: Verlag von Paul Parey, 1882.

Hawkes, Malcolm. *Russia/Chechnya: February 5: A Day of Slaughter in Novye Aldi.* Moscow: Human Rights Watch, June 2000.

Henze, Paul. *Chechnia: A Report of an International Alert Fact-Finding Mission.* September 24–October 3, 1992. London: International Alert, 1996.

——. "Marx on Russians and Muslims." *Central Asian Survey,* v. 6, no. 4 (1987).

Herbert, Agnes. *Casuals in the Caucasus: The Diary of a Sporting Holiday.* London: John Lane, Bodley Head, 1912.

The Ingush-Ossetian Conflict in the Prigorodnyi Region. New York: Human Rights Watch/Helsinki, May 1996.

Karny, Yo'av. *Highlanders: A Journey to the Caucasus in Quest of Memory.* New York: Farrar, Straus, and Giroux, 2000.

Layton, Susan. *Russian Literature and Empire: Conquest of the Caucasus from Pushkin to Tolstoy.* New York: Cambridge University Press, 1994.

Lermontov, Mikhail. *A Hero of Our Time,* tr. Paul Foote. London: Penguin Group, 1966.

Lieven, Anatol. *Chechnya: Tombstone of Russian Power.* New Haven: Yale University Press, 1998.

Longworth, John A. *A Year Among the Circassians.* London: Henry Colburn, 1840. 2 vols.

Maclean, Fitzroy. *To Caucasus, the End of All the Earth: An Illustrated Companion to the Caucasus and Transcaucasia.* London: Jonathan Cape, 1930.

Marsden, Philip. *The Spirit Wrestlers: A Russian Journey,* London: HarperCollins, 1998.

Mazaeva, Tamara. *100 Dnei Prezidenta.* Groznyi and Sankt-Peterburg: SEDA, 1997.

Musaev, Timur, and Zurab Todua. *Novaia Checheno-Ingushetia.* Moskva: Panorama, 1992.

Nichols, Johanna. *The Indigenous Languages of the Caucasus,* ed. Rieks Smeets. In *Northeast Caucasian Languages,* v. 4. Delmar, N.Y.: Caravan Books, 1994.

——. *Who Are the Chechen?* U.C. Berkeley Slavic Studies Bulletin, January 13, 1995.

Nivat, Anne. *Chienne de Guerre: A Woman Reporter behind the Lines of the War in Chechnya.* New York: PublicAffairs, 2001.

Orlov, Oleg, and Aleksandr Cherkasov. *Behind Their Backs: Russian Forces' Use of Civilians as Hostages and Human Shields during the Chechnya War,* ed. T. I. Kasatkina, tr. Paul LeGendre. Moscow: Memorial Human Rights Center, 1997.

Politkovskaya, Anna. *A Dirty War: A Russian Reporter in Chechnya,* ed. and tr. John Crowfoot. London: Harvill Press, 2001.

——. *A Small Corner of Hell: Dispatches from Chechnya.* Chicago: University of Chicago Press, 2003.

BIBLIOGRAPHY

Potto, V. A. *Kavkazskaia voina v otdel'nykh ocherkakh, epizodakh, legendakh i biografiiakh*. St. Petersburg: Tipografiia R. Golike, 1885–1891. 5 vols.

———. *Utverzhdenie russkogo vladychestva na Kavkaze*. Tiflis: Tipografiia Ia.K. Libermana, 1901–1904. 3 vols.

Rashid, Ahmed. *Taliban: Militant Islam, Oil and Fundamentalism in Central Asia*. New Haven: Yale Note Bene, 2002.

Slezkine, Yuri. "The USSR as a Communal Apartment, or How a Socialist State Promoted Ethnic Particularism," *Slavic Review*, v. 53, no. 2 (Summer 1994).

Smith, Sebastian. *Allah's Mountains: Politics and War in the Russian Caucasus*. London: I. B. Tauris and Co., Publishers, 1998.

Spencer, Edmund. *Travels in Circassia, Krim-Tartary, & C. Including a Steam Voyage down the Danube, from Vienna to Constantinople, and round the Black Sea*. London: Henry Colburn, 1839.

Stalin, J. V. *On the Road to Nationalism. (A Letter From the Caucasus.)* In *Works* [*Sochineniia*], v. 2. Moscow: Foreign Languages Publishing House, 1953.

Tishkov, Valery. *Chechnya: Life in a War-Torn Society*. Berkeley: University of California Press, 2004.

Lev Tolstoi. *Dnevniki (1847–1894), Sobranie sochinenii v dvadtsati dvukh tomakh*, v. 21. Moskva: Khudozhestvennaia literatura, 1985.

Tolstoy, Leo. *Hadji Murad*. In *Master and Man and Other Stories*, tr. Paul Foote. London: Penguin Group, 1977.

———. "A Prisoner of the Caucasus." In *How Much Land Does a Man Need? And Other Stories*, tr. Ronald Wilks. London: Penguin Group, 1993.

Trenin, Dmitri V., and Alesksei V. Malashenko, with Anatol Lieven. *Russia's Restless Frontier: The Chechnya Factor in Post-Soviet Russia*. Washington, D.C.: Carnegie Endowment for International Peace, 2004.

Whittock, Michael. "Ermolov–Proconsul of the Caucasus." *Russian Review*, v. 18, no. 1 (January 1959).

Wilson, A. N. *Tolstoy*. New York: W. W. Norton, 1988.

Yergin, Daniel. *The Prize: The Epic Quest for Oil, Money, and Power*. New York: Simon and Schuster, 1991.

Zelkina, Anna. *In Quest for God and Freedom: Sufi Responses to the Russian Advance in the North Caucasus*. London: C. Hurst & Co., 2000.

———. "Some Aspects of the Teaching of Kunta Hâjjî: On the Basis of the Manuscript by 'Abd al-Salâm Written in 1862 AD." *Journal of the History of Sufism*, no. 1–2 (2000).

ABOUT THE AUTHOR

Andrew Meier is the author of *Black Earth: A Journey Through Russia After The Fall*. (The *Economist* named *Black Earth* a "Book of the Year," and the New York Public Library selected it as one of the twenty-five "Books To Remember" for 2003.)

Fluent in Russian, Meier was a Moscow correspondent for *Time* from 1996 to 2001. A graduate of Wesleyan and Oxford universities, he has been a recipient of fellowships from the Woodrow Wilson International Center for Scholars in Washington, D.C. (2001–2002), and the Alicia Patterson Foundation for Journalism (1996). His writing on foreign affairs has also appeared in *Harper's*, the *Los Angeles Times*, the *New Republic*, the *New York Times*, and the *Washington Post*, among other publications. Meier has also reported and written for PBS television documentaries. A regular commentator on the BBC, CNN, and NPR, he lives with his wife and daughter in New York City.